L'Abbé Prévost

Twayne's World Authors Series
French Literature

David O'Connell, Editor

University of Illinois

TWAS 746

ANTOINE FRANÇOIS
PREVOST.

Né à Hesdin en Artois le 1.er Avril 1697 Mort près Chantilly le 23 Novembre 1763.

ANTOINE-FRANÇOIS PRÉVOST
(1697–1763)

L'Abbé Prévost

By Richard A. Smernoff

State University of New York, Oswego

Twayne Publishers • Boston

To a very special person, my wife Linda

*And to the memories
of Geraldine Brunell and the days of Wellesley
that long ago influenced my perception of Prévost*

L'Abbé Prévost

Richard A. Smernoff

Copyright© 1985 by G.K. Hall & Company
All Rights Reserved
Published by Twayne Publishers
A Division of G. K. Hall & Co.
A publishing subsidiary of ITT
70 Lincoln Street
Boston, Massachusetts 02111

Book Production by Elizabeth Todesco
Book Design by Barbara Anderson

Printed on permanent/durable acid-free
paper and bound in the United States of
America.

Library of Congress Cataloging in Publication Data

Smernoff, Richard A.
    L'Abbé Prévost.

    (Twayne's world author series. French literature; TWAS 746)
    Bibliography: p. 127
    Includes index.
    1. Prévost, Abbé, 1697–1763—Criticism and interpretation.
I. Title.   II. Series.
PQ2021.Z5S65   1985   843'.5   84–22522
ISBN 0-8057-6594-8

Contents

About the Author

Richard A. Smernoff is Professor of French at State University of New York at Oswego. He received a B.A. from Yale University, a *Certificat* from the Sorbonne, and his Ph.D. from Princeton University. While at Princeton he was the recipient of a Woodrow Wilson dissertation fellowship and later received a State University of New York Research Grant. Before coming to SUNY he taught at Smith College. He is the author of *André Chénier* in the Twayne World Authors Series and has written articles on Rousseau, Laclos, and Aragon in addition to reviewing for the *French Review*. His areas of interest include the Enlightenment, the French novel, and the absurd in twentieth-century French literature.

Preface

Two and one-half centuries have passed since des Grieux first gazed upon Manon Lescaut, the "sovereign" of his heart, an event that marked an important stage in the myth of passion as fatality, which the story of Tristan and Iseult had decreed. Although *Manon Lescaut* immediately attracted a wide following, many of Prévost's contemporaries regarded *Cleveland* as his most successful work whereas others believed that Prévost's fame would rest in his journal, *Le Pour et contre*. For generations of students in France and elsewhere, however, Prévost has been identified almost exclusively as the author of *Manon Lescaut* and as a pre-Romantic in an age largely dominated by rationalist philosophy. The popularity of the three operas based on the novel has done little to dispel this image and, as Peter Gay has pointed out, *Manon Lescaut* struck a responsive chord in the hearts of many eighteenth-century readers who approached Prévost on the most superficial level: "Sensibility all too often degenerated into sentimentality, and easy tears conveniently blinded the eyes of men and women reluctant to confront the realities of their times or their own lives."[1]

A number of studies during the past two decades on Prévost as well as on the Enlightenment in general and on the eighteenth-century novel have given us a more balanced appraisal of the priest-novelist, but Prévost remains an elusive figure.[2] The sheer volume of his output, his literary ambitions as novelist, journalist, editor, translator of British authors and the ancients, his work on the multivolume *Histoire générale des voyages,* and his activities as a Jesuit, Benedictine, and soldier have made it difficult at times to discern the unity of his work. Inasmuch, moreover, as disguises, abductions, duels, flights, and an infinite number of coincidences recur in his novels, critics have accused him of pandering to fashionable literary tastes while neglecting stylistic concerns. The tensions in Prévost's life, which in his first four decades manifested themselves in numerous shifts between the cloister and worldly society, seemed to give credence to the idea that the melodrama of his art was rooted in the melodrama of his life and that he must therefore be understood as an important popularizer of the expression of feeling in literature who nonetheless shared some of his century's worst excesses.

Prévost's work embodies the critical spirit of the Enlightenment, the desire to examine man in all his complexities in order to reach an understanding of human destiny and man's place in the universe. The magnitude of the endeavor, the eighteenth century's view of the *Encyclopédie* as the crowning achievement of man's ability to attain knowledge and the philosophes' bold pronouncements were but some of the characteristics of the age that seem to imbue it with an optimism bordering on arrogance.

Twentieth-century critics of the Enlightenment, however, have favored revisionist theories, emphasizing that the writers of the period proclaimed first and foremost the limitations of man's capacity to know and that this discovery was itself revelatory of knowledge, a primary truth from which all others had to emanate. In this respect Peter Gay has concluded that the very association of the eighteenth century with reason is a misnomer that distorts the spirit of the age.[3] The skepticism of the period translated itself into a rejection of all absolutes to define man and his world. For man in the Enlightenment was viewed as leading interdependent religious, moral, aesthetic, social, political, and economic lives in varying degrees of ascendancy at different times of his life. Noting that "current criticism has almost abolished the concept of the eighteenth century as an Age of Reason, optimistic and convinced of human progress in all spheres," Jean Perkins goes on to say that "as an age of transition the Enlightenment . . . produces a tension in its thought and creative works which may seem to be ambiguous at times."[4]

Prévost's work reflects this multiplicity. It is not only the number of pages he wrote that discourages any effort to reduce his thought to a single theory, for Laclos, essentially a one-novel author, has been equally inaccessible to many critics. In the case of Prévost the task of assessing his work is rendered more difficult by the fact that his protagonists are described at every age and in every circumstance, young men embarking on an apprenticeship of life in whom nascent passion collides with social constraints, clerics whose beliefs are tested by the ways of the world, philosophers who attempt to achieve a precarious balance between reason, faith, and feeling, and mature men who, bruised by the impossibility of totally penetrating another being's consciousness, are driven to sadism and self-destruction. The frenetic unfolding of events occurs in all corners of the world, and topical historical occurrences, such as the rise of Cromwell to power, the Jesuit-Jansenist controversy, and the citing of specific eighteenth-century Paris institutions, are interspersed with clearly fictional accounts. Scholars have seen classical, romantic, baroque, picaresque, and rococo elements in his work and Prévost remains at the center of all discussion concerning the evolution of *mémoires, histoires,* and *nouvelles* into the eighteenth-century novel.[5]

Prévost depicts man in every facet of his existence—recluse, adventurer, member of fashionable society, philosopher, criminal, and true believer. Like Voltaire, he suggests that all concepts of virtue and vice must be judged in terms of human contingencies. If there is a unity in Prévost, it lies perhaps in his rejection of all theories that propose definitive and absolute answers to questions concerning human nature and human destiny. The eminent scholar Jean Sgard has noted than an appreciation of Prévost as synthesizer is essential to an understanding of the Enlightenment and concludes that "the traditional opposition between a philosophical thought and a 'pre-Romantic' sensibility . . . has been especially unfortunate to an understanding of Prévost.[6]

Prévost reflects his age and, at the same time, illuminates the tradition of the humanist and moralist that has characterized every century of French literature. His inherent skepticism and perception of human instability and change recall Montaigne. His understanding of man's aversion to self-contemplation and need for diversion evokes Pascal. Prévost the psychologist foreshadows Proust's analysis of love's pathology whereas Prévost the chronicler of man's fundamental solitude and inability to control and understand his destiny anticipates the twentieth-century absurdists.

Despite the general renaissance of interest in Prévost, there does not exist at the present time a work in English that serves as an introduction to his entire collection of writings. It is my hope that this study will fill that gap and enable readers to see in Prévost's vast output the tensions inherent in the final stages of an old order, one that had existed since the Middle Ages and that had assigned generally understood meanings to such concepts as faith, honor, virtue, duty, feeling, society, and Providence, despite serious challenges during the Reformation and the Quarrel of the Ancients and the Moderns. Searching for happiness and for definitive insights into the workings of the universe, Prévost's characters are forced to live with uncertainties, which explains why the Prévostean novel is typically open-ended and inconclusive. This book is divided into eight chapters. The first chapter deals with Prévost's life and discusses at length his intellectual development, especially with respect to his experiences in England, his contributions as editor of *Le Pour et contre* and the *Histoire générale des voyages,* and his influence as a translator of English literature. In Chapter 2 I discuss the development of the eighteenth-century novel and in subsequent chapters the novels in chronological order. I have used the volumes of the new Grenoble edition of Prévost's work, edited by Jean Sgard, that were available at the time of my writing. With the exception of Mauzi's edition of *L'Histoire d'une Grecque moderne* and Coulet's Roissard edition of *Mémoires pour servir à l'histoire de Malte ou histoire de la jeunesse du commandeur de* ***, I have used the 1823 edition for other novels *(Campagnes philosophiques ou mémoires de M. de Montcal, Mémoires d'un honnête homme,* and *Le Monde moral).* All translations are my own.

I wish to express my appreciation to Anne Jones of the editorial department at G.K. Hall, David O'Connell, field editor of the Twayne World Authors Series, Lewis de Simone, manuscript editor, and Elizabeth Todesco, production editor, for their assistance in the preparation of this book.

Richard A. Smernoff

State University of New York, Oswego

Chronology

to be fulminated. 6 November, order for his arrest. 22 November, departure for England.

1729 Hired as tutor in Sir John Eyles's house in London.

1730 Travels in England with his pupil. Travels to Holland in the fall with the Chevalier de la Ravanne. Takes name Prévost d'Exiles. Works on *Cleveland* in Amsterdam.

1731 Announcement of forthcoming publication of Prévost's translation of the *Histoire du président de Thou*. March, first English edition in London of first two books of *Cleveland*. Volumes 5, 6, and 7 (*Manon Lescaut*) of the *Mémoires et aventures* appear in Amsterdam. Spring or summer, meets Lenki Eckhardt in The Hague. Maintains contact with her for the next ten years.

1732 Volumes 5 and 6 of the *Mémoires et Aventures* published in France by Didot.

1733 Prévost's furniture sold in The Hague by creditors. Returns to England with Lenki. Begins publishing *Le Pour et contre*. *Manon Lescaut* published in Rouen. October, *Manon* condemned to be burned by authorities. December, Prévost imprisoned in Gate House in London for having falsified a bank note in the name of Francis Eyles, his former student.

1734 Pardoned by Pope Clément XII. Returns to Paris.

1735 Volume 1 of *Le Doyen de Killerine*. Takes novitiate at the Abbey de la Croix-Saint-Leufroy near Evreux.

1736 Retained as Chaplain to the Prince de Conti.

1739 Continues work on *Cleveland* and *Le Doyen de Killerine*. Abandons work on *Le Pour et contre* for one year. Father dies in September.

1740 January, pressed by financial needs, offers services to Voltaire, who turns him down. Abandons definitively publication of *Le Pour et contre*.

1741 *Histoire d'une Grecque moderne; Mémoires pour servir à l'histoire de Malte ou histoire de la jeunesse du Commandeur de ***; Campagnes philosophiques ou mémoires de M. de Montcal; Histoire de Marguérite d'Anjou.*

1742   *Histoire de Guillaume le Conquérant* (historical romance). Returns to Paris.

1743   *Histoire de Ciceron*, translation of an English work.

1744   *Voyages du Capitaine Lade*.

1745   *Mémoires d'un honnête homme*.

1746   First volume of *Histoire générale des voyages*. Rents house at Chaillot.

1751   Abridged translation of Richardson's *Clarissa*.

1753   Translates Richardson's *Grandisson*. Definitive edition of *Manon Lescaut* printed by Didot in Paris.

1755   Succeeds Baron Friedrich Melchior von Grimm as editor of the *Journal Etranger* (January to September).

1759   Abandons work on *Histoire générale des voyages*.

1760   First two volumes of *Le Monde moral*. Works on a *Histoire de la maison de Condé et de Conti*.

1763   Dies of a stroke on 25 November.

1764   Volumes 3 and 4 of *Le Monde moral* published. Translation from the English of *Lettres de Mentor à un jeune seigneur*.

1783–1785   Edition of *Oeuvres choisies* in 39 volumes, Amsterdam.

Chapter One

The Life and Milieus of the Abbé Prévost

An investigation of the Abbé Prévost's life forces one to recognize the causal relationship between the century's two modes of existence, the expository and the clandestine. The first mode manifested itself in several ways. Letters were regarded not only as a means of communication but also as literary works to be preserved for future generations. The letter writer could of course dissimulate as much as he revealed, as Voltaire's *Correspondance* clearly indicates. Secondly, the interest in epistemology throughout the century was a key element in the age's self-revelatory posture, for the public expression of man's accumulated knowledge, culminating in the publication of Diderot's *Encyclopédie,* was considered to be as important as determining the limits of what man could know. In many ways the impetus behind Prévost's *Histoire générale des voyages* paralleled that of the *Encyclopédie.* Perhaps more than any other eighteenth-century phenomenon, however, the salons revealed the extremely tenuous relationship between truth and falsehood, for in their uneasy alliance between aristocratic worldly society and the artist the salons tended to blur distinctions between creative inspiration and the desire to please. Indeed, the very theatricality of the salons encouraged the formation of two separate personalities, one expressly revealed for public approval, the other submerged beneath layers of façade. Laclos's *Les Liaisons dangereuses* examines in detail the ramifications of such a schism. Although Prévost was not a true dévoté of salon society, he was clearly influenced by the ambiguous climate of Parisian society.

Two eighteenth-century figures, the Benedictine Dom Dupuis and the Chevalier de Ravanne, have left an extensive collection of material on the Abbé, but the accuracy of their statements is sometimes questionable. The work of Henry Harrisse, a nineteenth-century critic who undertook the task of assembling all known data on Prévost and annotating many of the sources, has been indispensable to twentieth-century critics of Prévost, including Engel, Roddier, and Sgard.[1]

Yet, despite Harrisse's contributions, Prévost remains an elusive figure.

Prévost's life has been paradoxically obscured by the very legend surrounding his fame as the author of one of the century's most popular works and by his status as ex-Jesuit, ex-Benedictine, ex-soldier, and ex-lover. The range of his activities and his mobility were characteristic of his age, yet although he knew both Voltaire and Rousseau, he was never considered a member of the Philosophic Party. Always aware of the power the censor could wield against him in the name of both the Crown and Rome, he was often forced to publish his works clandestinely. Remarks by Prévost on major issues of his life are not lacking, for he was not above using *Le Pour et contre* as a vehicle of personal expression, but his statements frequently assume the form of an apologetic. His tortuous efforts at self-definition, which define most consistently the nearly seven decades of his life, reveal what is perhaps the eighteenth century's most permanent legacy, the quest to define human nature.

The Early Years

Antoine-François Prévost was born in Hesdin in the province of Artois on 1 April 1697. The family had been in the region since the fifteenth century and the first Prévost mentioned in the archives of Hesdin was François, who died in 1651. Whereas the Prévosts of the sixteenth century were principally farmers or country priests, those of the seventeenth century were solidly bourgeois, assuming the functions of public administrators or entering either the monastic orders or the secular lay clergy. Prévost's paternal grandfather was an affluent brewer who became city treasurer and then was municipal magistrate for several terms.

As was customary for the sons of seventeenth-century bourgeois, many Prévosts entered the religious orders. Harrisse has noted at least fourteen relatives of the Abbé who were monks, priests, or nuns in the sixteenth and seventeenth centuries.[2] The family was equally well represented in magistrate positions. Hesdin was at this time a small village of Flemish character, industrious and bourgeois. Antoine's father, Liévin, born in 1666, was the king's counsellor and the public prosecutor of the bailiwick of Hesdin. He married Marie Duclay, a woman who bore him nine children, only five of whom reached adulthood. Two of Antoine's brothers were priests, Liévin-Norbert and Bernard-Joseph.

In 1711, following the death of both his mother and sister, Antoine, then fourteen years old, was sent by his father to the Jesuit College of Hesdin. In the course of the century the Jesuits were to alleviate some of the harsh conditions that had prevailed in their schools, but in 1711 the regime at Hesdin was very exacting. The sixteen-hour day was filled with study, prayers, and religious exercises and there was little time for recreation. The dates of Prévost's stay at Hesdin are controversial. Prévost claims to have left the Jesuits at the age of sixteen to bear arms. Harrisse believes that Prévost was a novice with the Jesuits in Paris from 1713 to 1714 and then transferred to the college of La Flèche in 1715 where one loses sight of his whereabouts after 1716.[3] There are few documents that relate to this period, but if we can believe what Prévost later wrote, this was not an unhappy time for him: "La Flèche and Saint-Germain where I lived are names that are dear to my memory."[4]

Prévost and the Jesuits. Since all of Prévost's uncles had been priests and his older brother Jérôme would inherit the paternal estate, it was natural that Antoine-François, too, should pursue a career in the Church. The Church in the eighteenth century was a microcosm of society in its diversity. The sons of great noblemen remained in outlook and way of life *grands seigneurs.* The secular clergy, by contrast, were frequently poorly paid and not very different in outlook from the peasants they served.[5]

The works of the ancients, especially Horace, Cicero, and Virgil, were an integral part of the Jesuit curriculum at this time. Prévost's depiction of Jesuits in his novels covers a broad spectrum. The intensity of his training may well have contributed to his interest in casuistry and in the moral and didactic novel. Like Voltaire, Prévost was to gain more fame as an ex-Jesuit than as a member of the order. Events in Prévost's life reveal that the Jesuits were no more successful in stifling his independence than they would be in their dealings with Voltaire.

The years of frenzied activity in which the Jesuit novice and youthful soldier made his way into the world to form another sort of apprenticeship are significant in two ways: they correspond to the general climate of society that characterized the years of the Regency and hint at the framework of some of Prévost's major novels, works in which young men, coming into their adulthood, discover within

themselves feelings and passions that are in conflict with earlier as-
similated values of honor and paternal authority. Although Prévost's
writings are neither biographies nor even strictly autobiographical,
the shape that his work would assume can be seen in embryonic form
from events of the first two decades of his life.

Following his brief period of military service, Prévost was once
again admitted as a novice to the Jesuits, this time at Rouen, on 11
March 1717. To be given the opportunity for a second novitiate was
a singular occurrence and suggests that his superiors had already
taken note of their charge's talents. In December of the same year
Prévost was at La Flèche for a second year of philosophy. Again his
stay was brief, for he left sometime in 1718 to serve in the army
again.

Prévost and Holland. Leaving La Flèche, Prévost made his
way to Holland. The evidence relating to this period of his life is
contradictory, but as one critic, Étienne Guilhou, has pointed out,
Prévost was frequently guilty of blatant hypocrisy and unquestionable
lying in his efforts to maintain a favorable image.[6] His repeated
change of plans undoubtedly conveyed an impression of instability
and aimlessness to his contemporaries. In his account of this period
Dom Depuis offers a different view, namely, that Prévost feared his
father's reprimands and traveled to Holland with a generous friend
who paid most of his expenses. In Holland Prévost was allegedly received in the best houses because of the reputation he was already beginning to enjoy in belles-lettres, which he enhanced by writing
several lively pieces in verse or in prose.

Prévost and the Benedictines. In 1719, about one year after
he left the Jesuits for a second time, Prévost once again asked to be
readmitted, but this time he was refused. In the following year he
was received by the Benedictines of the Congregation of St. Maur at
the Abbey of St. Wandrille near Rouen. In the eighteenth century
the Benedictines were not nearly as austere and given to self-denial as
commonly thought. The now-famous statement in which Prévost referred to his need to withdraw from society following an unhappy
love affair suggests that the order offered him an asylum where he
could attempt to reconcile conflicting elements in his character—a
passionate, sometimes impetuous need for mobility and a need for
analysis, a craving for lucidity and order which could be achieved
only during periods of calm reflection: "The unfortunate end of a too
tender involvement led me ultimately to the tomb. That is the name

which I give to the respectable order where I went to bury myself and where for a time I lived so truly dead that my family and my friends were ignorant of what I had become."[7]

The Benedictine Order was the oldest of all the monastic orders and had undergone several reforms over the centuries. The congregation of Saint-Maur in which Prévost sought refuge had been founded in 1621, was dedicated especially to scholarly works, and was probably most exempt from the general decadence that pervaded the monastic orders in the eighteenth century. Prévost's statement about renunciation of worldly pleasures cannot be taken too seriously. To enter a monastery at this time was to assure oneself of a peaceful existence and reasonable comfort.

On 9 November 1721, in the presence of his father, Prévost made a profession of faith at the Benedictine Abbey of Saint-Pierre de Jumièges. Dom Dupuis has referred to a rift between Liévin Prévost and his son because of the latter's challenge to parental authority in his indecisive moves between the Church, the military, and the world of pleasure. Harrisse, on the other hand, points to the ease with which Prévost became the victim of vicious gossip which claimed that he was guilty of parricide.[8] His independence and his insistence on his innocence in order to appear in the best possible light betray, nevertheless, a certain moral relativism that characterizes much of his personal thinking and the behavior of his major literary creations, including des Grieux, Patrice, and the diplomat of the *Histoire d'une Grecque moderne.* For all their casuistry, Prévost's words suggest that he viewed the diversity of his interests as proof of his singular character, thereby concluding that his actions should not be interpreted in terms of standards reserved for the common run of men: "I know the weakness of my heart and I feel how important it is for my peace of mind not to use it for sterile sciences which would cause it to wither up and languish; if I wish to be happy in Religion I must conserve in all its force the impression of grace which led me to it. . . ."[9]

Obviously Prévost's decision to enter the religious orders had little to do with a sense of vocation. Since religion, however, attempts to explain human destiny and the dualities of his personality led him increasingly to examine and assimilate all facets of human existence, Prévost could never divest himself entirely of the traditional values expressed in organized religion. Years after leaving the Benedictines he would write in *Le Pour et contre:* "Pleasures pass so quickly and satisfy so little . . . let us take as our lot the rewards of heaven which are certain rewards. Twenty or thirty years when I would suppose them spent in pleasures will not diminish the necessity of appealing to God one day. . . ."[10] In his remarks about the profession of faith he made to become a Benedictine, he revealed the thoroughly personal character of his concept of religion: "Heaven knows the depths of my heart, and that is enough to calm me . . . I pronounced the formula of my vows with all the interior restrictions that could authorize me to break them."[11]

Prévost remained in the Abbey de Saint-Ouen from 1722 to 1723, and in 1723 went to the Abbey de Notre-Dame-Du-Bec to study theology. During this time he was preparing a work that appeared in 1724, *Les Aventures de Pomponius, chevalier romain, ou l'histoire de notre temps* (The adventures of Pomponius, a Roman Knight, or the history of our times), an anti-Regent work written in a style that already evokes des Grieux's impassioned plea that love be understood as a natural passion: "Love was his failing, if indeed it is one; because one must confess that this passion has something so sweet and so natural that one doesn't need to be an epicurean to love."[12]

Séez and Saint-Germain-des-Près.   Seventeen twenty-six was an important year in Prévost's life. He began teaching humanities at the Collège de Saint-Germer and fulfilled his desire to be ordained a priest. Soon after he was sent to Evreux for one year (1726–1727) because the inhabitants of that city needed a priest during Lent. From this point on Prévost moved frequently. Having already lived in the Abbey at Notre-Dame-du Bec in Normandy, he also had brief associations with two other abbeys in the province, in Fécamp and Séez. It was at Séez that he began work on the last volume of the *Histoire de M. de Thou* (The history of M. de Thou), which had been left unfinished by the death of the canon at Séez, M. du Pont. The privilege of nurturing his literary talent was revoked by the Benedictines as soon as he finished his work on de Thou.

Sgard views each of the stages in Prévost's religious life as a new milestone in his literary career but adds that this integration of Prévost's many interests was precarious inasmuch as it was linked to clandestinity.[13] The circumstances surrounding the publication of the novels of the 1730s shed light on the kinds of obstacles with which the writer had to contend. It is true that the economic position of men of letters and their status in society underwent a vast improvement in the course of the century. Writers still had to struggle, however, with a limited reading public, and the publisher who acquired a manuscript was faced with the certainty that if the book was a success the sales of his edition would be greatly reduced by pirated editions produced both at home and abroad. Publishers themselves were frequently unscrupulous in their dealings with authors who resorted to duplicity and anonymity to protect their interests. The question of the novel and the public's craving for authentic *mémoires* will be examined in a later chapter.

After his stay in Séez Prévost was sent to Paris in April 1727 and it was here, Harrisse believes, that he began to write the *Mémoires et aventures d'un homme de qualité qui s'est retiré du monde* (Memoirs and adventures of a man of quality who has withdrawn from the world). [14]

Whereas Prévost initially regarded the move to Paris as a favor, his pleasure turned to indignation when he came to feel that he was being scrutinized and that his supervisors wished to limit his independence. No longer a novice, he was not prepared to underestimate his own worth. The pattern of his religious life, which involved brief stays in a number of monasteries, had become firmly established. In 1728 he was once again transferred, this time to Saint-Germain-des-Près.

The abbey, with its great tower, walls, and trenches still resembled a citadel but was celebrated for its intense intellectual life. Its Benedictines, preparing new Greek and Latin editions of the works of the Church fathers, were engaged in scholarly research everywhere through a network of correspondence which frequently necessitated traveling. They enjoyed a universal reputation. The chief work of the abbey at the time of Prévost's arrival was the editing of the *Gallia Christiana,* enormous works composed by a team of researchers. The youngest monks copied notes and translated into Latin what others had written in French. Prévost's frustration at being assigned work that required little creative imagination is suggested by the many scathing portraits of members of this order that appear in the third volume of the *Mémoires d'un homme de qualité.* In a letter written on 18 October 1728 to his superior, Dom Thibault, Prévost expressed unequivocally his discontentment with his life, insisted that his behavior had always been beyond reproach, and declared the anguish he had undergone at being regarded with suspicion by the other members of the congregation. [15] A growing dissatisfaction with the routine and discipline of monastic life led to his request for a transfer to a less rigorous branch of the order. Prévost was granted a *bref de translation,* a short document that contained the Pope's instructions relative to a specific individual. In order for the *bref* to be legal, however, it had to be fulminated, that is, made public by Prévost's superior. Prévost did not wait for the fulmination and left the abbey, trading his monk's robe for a priest's collar. The fact that he continued to wear a habit suggests that he had no intention of breaking openly with the Church but that, typically and naively, he had interpreted his vows in a very personal way and had never regarded them as absolutely binding. When he learned that a *lettre de cachet* had been issued against him he decided to go to England. And so, on 22 November 1728, Prévost set sail for a country that had been favored by the French since the beginning of the century.

Prévost and England

The England of 1728 was a center of intellectual activity. Voltaire had arrived there only two years earlier and Montesquieu in 1727. The Protestants, fleeing a France that had revoked the Edict of Nantes, had found a haven in England. The number of Anglophiles was growing yearly among French intellectuals, who regarded England as the embodiment of civility and human liberty. England was later to attract political conservatives as well in the person of the royalists who sought refuge there during the Revolution.

The influence of England in Prévost's intellectual development is undeniable. One of his major novels is titled *Le Philosophe anglais, ou histoire de Monsieur Cleveland* (The English philosopher, or History of Monsieur Cleveland), and one of the later works, the *Mémoires de M. de Montcal* (Memoirs of M. de Montcal), concerns the adventures of a French Protestant engaged in military service in England. *Le Pour et contre,* which began publication in 1733, reveals the extent of Prévost's interest in English institutions and culture and his translations of Samuel Richardson's novels were widely read. Sgard views the years 1718, 1728, and 1736 as milestones in Prévost's life because he believes that they represent respectively three stages of his break with the past: Regency thought, English thought, and philosophical thought. Prévost's experiences in England, his association with Voltaire and with Dutch freethinkers all contributed, in Sgard's view, to Prévost's evolution away from the "shadows" toward the principles of the new thought with which he was in basic agreement. [16]

Prévost was obviously sensitive to the fact that the climate of daily life in England provided greater freedom to the writer, for his letters indicate that he valued English customs and literary traditions highly. On the other hand, it is clear that his experiences in England and his interest in current events and the contemporary literary scene did not lead him to break openly with the fundamental ideas of his classical formation, which included the study of the ancients.

It is known that Prévost applied himself very diligently to learning the English language and to familiarizing himself with English customs.[17] He was thus able to penetrate English society actively and was not forced to limit his knowledge of the country to books. Through his efforts to learn English he was able to participate in the literary life of England by attending plays and making numerous excursions. In London he became the tutor of Francis Eyles, son of Sir John Eyles, a former director of the Bank of England and a Lieutenant Governor of the South Seas Company. This association helped defray Prévost's expenses and also provided him with the opportunity to travel extensively through the south of England.

An account in the *Mémoires et aventures d'un homme de qualité,* which appears to be largely autobiographical, suggests that Prévost traveled to Turnbridge and Bath as well as Hastings, Portsmouth, Southhampton, Plymouth, Bristol, Oxford, Windsor, and then back to London. Later he mentions passing through Canterbury, thus completing an itinerary that took him through virtually the entire southern part of the country. Prévost observed English life, then, not from the vantage point of a foreigner who judges from afar, but rather as one who attended masked balls, boxing matches, and theatrical events.

His training at the colleges at Hesdin and La Flèche had been heavily steeped in the Latin classics. He admired many seventeenth-century authors, especially Racine, La Bruyère, and Fénelon. Despite his having received a Jesuit education that emphasized the classics, he maintained a moderate position with respect to the Quarrel of the Ancients and the Moderns, expressing not only a reverence for the ancients but also a respect for Montaigne's relativism and Fontanelle's knowledge of the sciences. Prévost's enthusiastic appreciation of the English attitude toward individual liberties is reminiscent of many of Voltaire's statements in the *Lettres philosophiques.* Prévost recognized that the spirit of tolerance that pervaded many sectors of English society was the result of careful education and therefore had to be nur-

tured: "There is no country where one finds so much honesty, so
much humanity, ideas so rife with honor, wisdom, and happiness as
among the English."[18]

The Conversion to Protestantism. The dignity and freedom
that Prévost enjoyed in England contrasted with the restrictions he
had known as a member of the orders. Sgard has observed that in
England Prévost became what he desired, not a fugitive but a man of
quality who found a place for himself in the prominent Eyles family.[19] During this period, according to Holzbecher, one of his contemporaries, Prévost fell in love with one Pegg D., shared a secret
promise of marriage to her, and converted to Anglicanism. If the con-
versions alluded to are true, one can assume that this period of
Prévost's life contributed in a very personal way to his depiction of
the numerous evolutions that his character Cleveland undergoes. It
seems fairly certain in the light of Prévost's own statements on his
religious vows that his conversion to Protestantism did not involve
any kind of doctrinal or liturgical commitment. His actions here were
typically motivated by expediency, and one can believe that any vows
he took to embrace the Anglican faith were made in the same spirit
of independence that characterized his entrance into the Catholic religious orders.

Prévost's first visit to England lasted nearly two years. The enthu-
siasm with which he spoke of his experiences suggests that he was
able to reconcile his former life as a cloistered scholar with that of the
practical citizen: "The English have recognized that constraint is an
attack against the spirit of the Bible. They know that the heart of
man is the domain of God; that violence produces only external
changes."[20]

Lenki and *Manon Lescaut*

Some time in the fall of 1730 Prévost abruptly left England for
Holland where he took the name Prévost d'Exiles. The Chevalier de
Ravanne wrote that a love affair was responsible for this hasty departure. Henri Roddier believes that Sir John Eyles looked unfavorably
upon his tutor's setting a bad example for his son.[21] In any event Ravanne accompanied Prévost to Holland where they went from Rotter-
dam to the Hague and then to Amsterdam. Thus, within a two-year
period Prévost had contact with two European capitals widely known

for granting refuge to foreigners and to facilitating the dissemination of liberal ideas.

Although Prévost did not penetrate Dutch society to the extent that he integrated himself into English life, his creative activity showed little sign of slowing down, for it was in Holland that he worked on four volumes of *Cleveland*. He also became entangled during this period with the infamous Lenki Eckhardt, described by Ravanne as a bloodsucker because of her material demands on Prévost and thought for a time to have been a model for Manon. Harrisse has ascertained, however, that the manuscript for the *Histoire du Chevalier des Grieux et de Manon Lescaut* was already complete when Prévost first came to London and that he waited until he was assured of the popularity of the earlier volumes of the novel before he had it published.[22] There is little doubt that Prévost's affair with Lenki increased his financial problems. He thus contracted to publish regularly scheduled volumes of the new novel he was writing, *Cleveland*. By October 1731 the first four books had appeared, but by 1732 he was unable to fulfill his contract obligations with the result that in January 1733 his furniture was sold in The Hague as partial payment to his creditors.

Le Pour et contre

The exact date of Prévost's return to England is uncertain, but it is thought that he was back in London with Lenki by March 1733 if not in January. Although his financial embarrassment was probably more the result of poor judgment than conscious maliciousness, he was infamous in Holland as a swindler. Almost immediately upon returning to England Prévost began publishing *Le Pour et contre*. It was printed in Paris and approved on 17 July 1733. In London Prévost had firsthand contact with a free and popular newspaper in which social, political, religious, and literary issues, as well as issues of the day, were discussed. The climate of freedom that prevailed in England attracted him. Such were the circumstances of his life in 1733—the flight from Holland, the bankruptcy and the ensuing scandal, the battles with publishers—that the only bookseller with whom he could maintain any relations was François Didot in Paris. Prévost wrote that his aim was to incorporate into his project all that belongs to the domain of letters. Prévost's undertaking was not as uncomplicated as one might suspect. The name of the journal, *Le Pour et contre, journal littéraire d'un goût nouveau* (The pros and the cons, a literary journal in a new vein), suggests a polemical character and the title page, which appeared at the beginning of every volume, upheld the principle of nonpartisanship:

The *Pour et contre,* a periodical journal in a new taste in which one expresses oneself freely on everything that can interest the curiosity of the Public in matters of Science, the Arts, Books, Authors, and without taking any sides and without offending anyone.[23]

References made by Prévost to this journal as a *feuille littéraire* indicate that he regarded it first and foremost as a literary journal. At the same time he wished to avoid imitating the existing publications of the day. His would not be as serious as the *Journal des sçavans* nor would it adopt the format of the *Mercure de France,* which maintained a rigorous plan throughout. The *Pour et contre* would be a chronicle written from day to day in which critical comments on works of the past would be juxtaposed with current anecdotes, extracts taken from English authors, including plays and *récits de voyages;* in short, all that would reveal to the French hitherto unknown aspects of "the genius of the English, the curiosities of London and other parts of the island, the progress made daily there in the sciences and arts, and even to translate sometimes the most beautiful scenes of their dramatic literature."[24]

Despite the restrictions imposed by French authorities—approval for publication of the first issue was granted only after the removal of "references to ecclesiastical matters"—Prévost's first issues revealed his originality both in content and style as he described various aspects of English civilization. Not wishing to imitate the technique of the English satirists, he attempted to grasp the fundamental principles of Bayle's *Dictionnaire* in which irony was tempered with erudition and humor with sensitivity to exactness of expression. The influence of La Bruyère's art of portraiture and Fénelon's use of dramatic narrative is evident throughout. Prévost envisaged his publication as a sociological experiment in cultural relativity whereby he would contrast French and English judgments on the same works in order to show differences of taste. A portion of the topics covered in the twenty volumes of the *Pour et contre* indicates the scope of the undertaking, notwithstanding the fact that Prévost avoided most discussion of matters related to religion and politics:[25]

1. The State of the Sciences and the Arts
2. New Works in Any Genre
3. Newspapers
4. Manners and Customs of the Century
5. Common Prejudices
6. The Character of Illustrious Men
7. Comparison of Great Men
8. The Character of Women Distinguished by Merit
9. New Establishments
10. New Medals
11. Extraordinary Inventions of Art

Prévost's criticism of English authors was guided by his belief that one must be thoroughly familiar with the milieu and character of a people in order to understand its literature. He thus tended to adhere to Montaigné's principle that everything in morals as well as in literature is relative and not absolute. Despite his desire to please his readers, he was perhaps most concerned with familiarizing the French with other modes of thought. His criticism of English authors is more restrained than that shown by Voltaire in the *Lettres philosophiques,* in part because Prévost had a better grasp of the English language than did Voltaire. Prévost's conclusions on Shakespeare typify his approach to literature. He was not uncritically enthusiastic toward Shakespeare as were many English writers, yet he did not share the French critics' indignant hostility toward this playwright. The question of the ancients versus the moderns was no longer a burning issue when Prévost began publishing *Le Pour et contre.* It had been supplanted by a new movement in the history of ideas that pitted Cartesians against Newtonians. To a certain extent the partisans in this debate were influenced by feelings of national pride.[26]

Prévost's vocation, as Sgard has stated, was that of an intermediary.[27] He analyzed at length differences of taste, studied adaptations of French plays on the English stage and the value of translations from English into French. His literary bent allowed him to transcribe contemporary English events into anecdotes that informed his French readers of current events in England while entertaining them. Prévost's pronouncements on aesthetic matters, his interest in contrasting French and English customs, his ability to distinguish universal principles of taste among the qualities relative to a particular age bear the concerns of a moralist. Perhaps no writer could have fulfilled all the ambitious goals that Prévost set out for himself in *le Pour et contre,* but, as Sgard has noted, this period remains the "most complete witness that Prévost left on himself."[28]

Because of delays, changes of editors, and periods when publication was suspended, the journal did not appear regularly. One volume appeared in 1733, three in 1734, two in 1735, three in 1736, four in 1737, two in 1738, two in 1739, and three in 1740.

In its conception, execution, and influence *Le Pour et contre* represented the kind of literary cosmopolitanism that was entirely in keeping with the Enlightenment spirit. As a vehicle for the expression of new ideas it added another moderate voice to the ancients-moderns controversy of the preceding century in its assumption that taste, excellence, and the very concept of progress have no temporal or geographical limitations. Its ramifications were very great indeed, for it brought daily life in England to the attention of the French in a much more accessible form than had the writings of Voltaire and other Frenchmen of the period. After *Le Pour et contre* England was no longer an unknown haven of liberty but an island whose institutions, customs, and civilization were depicted realistically, a country which, as the days of the Revolution would bear out, was as capable of granting refuge to conservative royalists as to those fleeing the power of the monarchy earlier in the century.

Prévost and Voltaire

Prévost and Voltaire were drawn together because of *Le Pour et contre.* Sgard believes that the two writers' intellectual affinities and similarities of taste led them to a collaboration on a critique of Voltaire's *Eléments de la philosophie de Newton.*[29] Sgard's views do not differ essentially from those of René Pomeau, who has also written about the relationship of the two men.[30] In a more recent article, however, Steve Larkin has refuted the claims made of an extended collaboration between Voltaire and Prévost, stating that unjustified assumptions have been made about the identity of "Le Prévost" designated in Voltaire's correspondence, and even questioning, in the absence of irrefutable evidence, whether the writers ever met.[31]

In the light of the evidence it seems fairly conclusive that the relationship of the authors centered almost exclusively about their recognition that *Le Pour et contre* could be used to serve their own interests, in Voltaire's case as a vehicle to defend him against the attacks of enemies and for Prévost the chance to establish his journal as a serious, well-informed, and topical literary review, which led him therefore to devote extensive sections of numbers 11, 12, and 13 to Voltaire's *Lettres philosophiques*.

Prévost's interest in English sciences and philosophy was decidedly more peripheral than Voltaire's. In Larkin's view Voltaire never attempted to enlist Prévost in the *lutte philosophique* because he recognized that the views and interests of the period's most prolific novelist—and Voltaire did not conceal his disdain for the novel as a literary genre—were too different from his own to be of any importance to him.[32] In 1738 Voltaire had reproached Prévost for not coming to his defense when the Abbé Desfontaines had published his scathing attack on him in a pamphlet entitled *La Voltairomanie*. Early in 1740 Prévost wrote to Voltaire and offered to be of assistance to him in writing a *Défense de M. de Voltaire et de ses ouvrages*.[33] In the course of his letter it becomes clear that Prévost was not motivated by altruism. He went on to explain that his debts amounted to fifty louis and asked if Voltaire could spare him "the most cruel embarrassment" by virtue of "his generosity and zeal for men of letters." Responding five months later, Voltaire rejected Prévost's offer but proposed instead to recommend him to the court of Berlin. Although the two men frequently arrived at the same conclusions concerning human nature and man's future—there are examples of striking parallels in situations and conclusions that occur in Voltaire's *contes* and Prévost's novels—they formed a relationship in which intellectual affinities were secondary to professional interest. Not surprisingly, Voltaire's opinion of Prévost rose considerably as a result of Prévost's having allowed Voltaire to answer his detractors in a long letter that appeared in a 1738 issue of *Le Pour et contre*.

Scandal, Flight, and Return to the Orders

Le Pour et contre had appeared for only a few months when scandal again touched Prévost's life. In December 1733 he was jailed for having forged a bill of exchange for fifty pounds in the name of his former pupil, Francis Eyles. Ravanne explains the incident as another example of Lenki's leading Prévost astray because of her financial demands on him whereas Harrisse contends that Ravanne had not returned to London after 1731 and therefore could not have personal knowledge of Prévost's activities.[34] In a curious juxtaposition of life and art, in which the fortunes of the young des Grieux pursuing Manon paralleled those of his creator, Prévost was being attacked in Paris in the same month of his arrest on the grounds of his having written an immoral book, the *Histoire du Chevalier des Grieux et de Manon Lescaut*. Prévost's name was besmirched in a series of vitriolic outcries by Mathieu Marias, the President of the Lawyers in Parliament who, while admitting that the book and the author had style, recommended, nonetheless, that both be burned.[35]

Because of the forged note, Prévost thought it best to leave London, and during the first months of 1734 he once again began working on obtaining a pardon in Paris from his former Benedictine superiors. Since leaving Paris in 1728 he had tried to maintain friendly relations with the order. Writing to Dom Clément de la Rue from The Hague on 10 November 1731, he had again evoked a posture that foreshadowed Rousseau's tone in his *Confessions,* an appeal to his personal morality and knowledge of right and wrong: "Heaven knows the depths of my heart, that is enough to give me peace."[36]

Prévost's return to France early in 1734 marked an improvement in his fortunes. In June of that year Pope Clement XII pardoned him and accorded him a *bref de translation* for another branch of the Benedictines without ever mentioning the abbé's conversion to Protestantism. On 11 September the brief was fulminated. Prévost now had the opportunity to reenter the religious life in France. Early in February 1735 he was assigned to the Abbey de la Grenetière near Nantes, but upon his request was subsequently assigned to the Abbey de la Croix-Saint-Leufroy near Evreux in a region where he had apparently made some friends. One of the conditions of his reintegration into the orders was the taking of another novitiate. A letter written during the same period from the Abbé Le Blanc to Président Bouhier indicates that Prévost's novels, activities as a religious, and journalism had conferred a kind of celebrity status on him.[37] Prévost's writings during this period suggest that he was not unhappy. In an August issue of *Le Pour et contre* he spoke of his solitude but wrote later that he found the company of the dukes and duchesses charming. By November he was complaining to his friend Thiériot that he was obliged to stay in the Abbey until 10 December.[38] When he returned to Paris in the middle of winter (1736) he was named *aumônier,* or chaplain, to the Prince de Conti.

After years of exile, of financial insecurity, and a nomadic existence, the Abbé Prévost d'Exiles returned to Paris as a celebrated figure. He now had the reputation of a man who passed with equal ease in the milieus of both the cloisters and worldly society. His exploits and personality seemed to make of him a larger-than-life figure, one who was capable of showering his friends with generosity while swindling his editors. The first four decades of his life suggest a personality type that, named after Goethe's prototype, would be known as Faustian. No one single mode of existence dominated Prévost's life during these years. The monastery was for him an asylum from the ways of man rather than a sanctuary for contemplation of metaphysical truths. A prolific writer who was capable of a prodigious output, he craved the company of exotic women but only insofar as he could maintain his independence. Numerous geographical changes reflecting inner emotional turmoil influenced the rhythm of these years, yet there is one overriding quality, the need for self-definition and self-justification and an implicit breakdown between intent and action, that foreshadows Rousseau's spiritual journey. Like Jean-Jacques, Voltaire, Diderot, and so many of the age, Prévost was an exacting spectator in the drama of his own life.

Brussels and Frankfurt

The relative calm that Prévost knew in Paris under the Prince de Conti's protection was interrupted in January 1741 when he was named as an accomplice by a gazeteer for having altered certain pages of material published in the journal. Prévost spent most of 1741 outside of France. He first fled to Brussels where he was warmly greeted and "furnished with all the necessary and pleasant things" in order to avoid the infamous *lettre de cachet* that had been issued against him.[39] By the middle of October he was in Frankfurt where, in a letter dated 9 November 1741 to Cachaumont, he again expressed his desire to return to France where "things will be very favorable for me in my family."[40] Prévost reports in the same letter that Lenki, who had become Madame de Chester in 1734, had recently become Madame Dumas. Roddier suggests that Prévost maintained regular contact with Lenki throughout the 1730s and attributes his prolific output from

1738 to 1741 to his constant need for money "to live with Mme de Chester the life of a Man of Quality."[41]

Translations of Richardson's Novels

The last twenty-two years of Prévost's life were among the most prolific. Toward the end of 1741 he settled down with his relatives in Frankfurt and was back in Paris by September 1742. He had devoted a considerable number of pages in *Le Pour et contre* to translating into French the works of English authors such as John Dryden's *All for Love,* Richard Steele's *Conscious Lovers,* and Alexander Pope's *On the Art of Sinking in Poetry.* These imperfect translations are significant, however, inasmuch as they provided an apprenticeship for Prévost's translations of Richardson's novels. Like Montesquieu and Voltaire, Prévost was intensely interested in English culture and society, suggesting in *Le Pour et contre* that taste and other traits that contribute to the spirit of a people are the result of complex sociological factors that are neither objective nor static: "I write nothing that I do not have before my eyes." Prévost had underscored the need for open-mindedness in acknowledging cultural differences: "It is certain that each nation has its particular character of genius and expression."[42]

It is not known if Prévost was the translator of the four-volume edition of *Pamela* that appeared in 1742, but there is no doubt that he translated *Clarissa* (1751) and *Grandisson* (1753).[43] It was the treatment of realism in Richardson that most interested Prévost, particularly scenes of domestic life. Scenes of parents plotting to influence their children's future marriages and the gradual revelation of the individual's complex psychology appear in Prévost's translations. The idealism of *Grandisson* had an apparent impact on Rousseau who similarly explored the conflicts between passion and virtue in *La Nouvelle Héloïse.* Prévost took major liberties in his translations because Richardson, envisioning the novel on the highest moral plane, felt that it had to reflect Christian doctrines. Prévost had no hesitations about omitting whole sections when he felt that his readers would lose interest if he included them. The Richardson who emerges from these pages reflects a French sensibility, yet Prévost played an essential role in revealing to the French the bourgeois lyricism that was Richardson's unique contribution. For Rousseau and other Frenchmen who exulted in Richardson's powerful eloquence and use of the novel to express conflicts of contemporary society, but who would have been either unwilling or unable to read Richardson's voluminous tomes, the translations of Richardson's novels, capturing the essential spirit if not the form of Richardson's vision, are a noteworthy achievement in Prévost's artistic life.

The *Histoire génerale des voyages*

The *Histoire générale des voyages,* Prévost's lengthiest work, which first appeared in 1746, reveals the scope of his ambition as well as his concept of history as a fusion of man's biological evolution with his social, political, cultural, and religious transformations. In 1744 Prévost had published the *Voyages de Robert Lade* in which he imposed a fictitious story on descriptions of real voyagers. The *Histoire générale des voyages,* whose publication Prévost directed until 1759, exemplifies the encyclopedic spirit of the age. In one sense the motivation behind this project was not entirely original, for there existed numerous *récits de voyages* in which individual geographical discoveries and explorations were celebrated. Prévost's enterprise differed in its scope. It was to be a "complete system of history and modern geography, which will represent the current state of all nations."[44] Geography for Prévost was not limited to land formation and agriculture but included the customs of a people—their religion, government, arts, sciences, and commerce—that contribute to their uniqueness. Thus his broad concept of geography was directly related to a theory of relativity similar to that which Montesquieu had formulated in *De l'esprit des lois.*

The impetus behind the work was related to the unanswered questions of the previous century that had surfaced in the Quarrel of the Ancients and the Moderns. As one who had lived among the Jesuits and Benedictines, Prévost understood in 1746 what André Chénier was to assert in "L'Invention," that the theory of progress cannot be applied to creative works of art and that each age has its geniuses.

The *Histoire générale des voyages,* the most widely read of Prévost's works during his lifetime, is of critical importance because it enabled him to project an image of himself that coincided with his highest intellectual aspirations, that of a messenger of light. Financially rewarding, the publication allowed Prévost to amplify his investigation into the human heart. In the *Histoire générale des voyages* the Jesuit-educated writer and the moralist became one. Michèle Duchet sees Prévost's concept of history mirroring that of his century since Montesquieu. The human drama throughout the ages was the result neither of providence nor of chance, but rather of a system of forces, a linking of causes and effects, and the inexorable judgment of time which confers power on the strongest and the most daring.[45] These voyages were never conceived by Prévost as isolated events but rather as a source of historical and geographical knowledge. Prévost's writings juxtaposed authentic narratives of voyages with the theme of escape, flight, and the desire for the exotic and unknown, the material of the romantic literary imagination.

The Last Years

By September 1740 Prévost was well situated in Paris and was hard at work in translating a History of Cicero from the English. New works appeared in rapid succession: *Mémoires pour servir à l'histoire de Malte, ou histoire de la jeunesse du commandeur de ****, Amsterdam, 1741, *Campagnes philosophiques, ou mémoires de M. de Montcal*, Amsterdam, 1741; *Histoire d'une Grecque moderne*, Amsterdam, 1741; and *Histoire de Guillaume le Conquérant*, Paris, 1742.

At the age of forty-nine, having secured a reputation as a widely read novelist, translator, and editor of journals, Prévost now assumed a role resembling that of an elder statesman, an established *homme de lettres* whose improved financial situation and reputation contrasted with the years spent in exile where frequent moves reflected not only geographical changes but shifting worldly experiences. In his letter to Bouhier d'Etang, Prévost writes that "sooner or later sensible men form a penchant for solitude. They lose too much living beyond themselves."[46] Yet, despite his declared intentions Prévost never completely severed his worldly connections. Having leased a house for three years at Chaillot in 1746 where in a letter he speaks of the pleasures of life with his housekeeper Loulou, his cook, and his valet, he continued to frequent the salons of Mme Doublet and the Marquise de Créquy and received a small group of friends, including Voltaire's niece Mme Denis and Boulanger, the author of *Le Despotisme Oriental*.[47] Rousseau speaks in his *Confessions* of having met Prévost, referring, according to Harrisse, to an event of 1750. Speaking of the gathering, Rousseau writes: "At their head I place the Abbé Prévost, a very likable and very simple man, whose heart invigorates the writings, worthy of immortality, and who had nothing either in his disposition or in his company resembling the somber tones he gives to his works."[48]

Rousseau's vision in *La Nouvelle Héloïse* is clearly more idealistic than Prévost's, for it contains little of the human depravity that characterizes the world of *Cleveland*. In his personal life, however, Prévost seemed to exemplify the semi-withdrawal from society in which he had placed Cleveland at the end of the narrative. Rousseau could perhaps sense during the meeting that the creator of Renoncour and Cleveland had come to believe that happiness could be found most readily in the simplicity of a virtuous life which allowed the individual to maintain his independence.

The success of the *Histoire générale des voyages* alone would have prevented Prévost from leading a life of retreat, for the work was so successful that it had three editions in one year and was translated into German. As envisaged by Prévost, the voyage was an integral part of the science of man. Prévost's work on this publication reflected the new sociology as seen in three other seminal works of the century: Rousseau's *Discours sur les origines de l'inégalité* (Discourse on the origins of inequality), Voltaire's *Essai sur les moeurs* (Essay on mores), and Buffon's *Histoire Naturelle* (Natural history). Billy bases his contention that the *Histoire générale des voyages* contributed more to Prévost's reputation than the novels on the fact that for more than a century the *Voyages* was the primary source of all the knowledge of European readers on overseas countries.[49]

Prévost's involvement with the *Journal étranger,* whose editorship he assumed in 1755, illustrates further the breadth of his interests. The aim of the journal was to promote the development of a cosmopolitan spirit among the peoples so that they might live in greater harmony: ". . . to naturalize as it were reason in all peoples and confer on it everywhere a certain universality which it seems to still lack."[50]

The last few years of Prévost's life are obscure inasmuch as there are few primary sources in existence. In all probability Prévost renewed his lease at Chaillot. In 1754 Pope Benedict XIV furnished him with a priory in the diocese of Le Mans. Taking possession of this property in September of that year, he continued to work on the *Histoire des voyages* for five more years. In 1739 his father died and between 1742 and the time of his death in 1763 three of his brothers died. From documents collected by Harrisse we know that Prévost spent most of his last months (1762–1763) at Saint-Firmin in Chantilly where he worked on a *Histoire de la maison de Condé et de Conti,* unfinished at the time of his death. Prévost had been named chaplain to the Prince de Conti in 1736. To be named historiographer of an illustrious family was an even more flattering sign of recognition.

Despite the unqualified success of the *Histoire générale des voyages* and the continuing popularity of many of Prévost's works, the abbé's last years were not free of financial insecurity. For amidst the outwardly idyllic existence of Chaillot, Le Mans, and Chantilly, he continued to be at the mercy of booksellers who never ceased to hound him with contract deadlines and threats. To the end Prévost maintained his taste for women. At the end of 1762, confined to Chantilly, he set up conjugal living arrangements with his governess, Madame de Genty, the daughter of a haberdasher, who, far from being rich, added to his financial burden. She outlived Prévost by thirty years and to the end honored his memory.

During the last years of his life Prévost occasionally left Chantilly to go to Paris only some twenty-five miles away, but rarely stayed there for any period of time. Participating in the Prince de Conti's festivals and diversions, he was also involved in religious writings to which he attached the greatest importance. A few years before his death he emerges as a man whose attachment to religion is based more on the morality of religion, a religion of feeling, than on strict observance of formal dogma: "Nothing," he wrote, "has ever diminished the veneration that I have for the Christian faith. I mean that which . . . orders the love of God and that of one's neighbor."[51]

When Prévost died on 25 November 1763 of a stroke, he was one of the most widely known writers in Europe, an artist in whose vision the moralist, sociologist, poet, and psychologist became inextricably linked. The very sense of the incommensurate, of the absurd, that forms the matrix of his narratives was underscored by the inscription on his gravestone, for here he was unceremoniously described as Dom Antoine Prévost, priest and monk of the Order of St. Benedict who was known for the large number of books he had written.

Chapter Two

The French Novel in the Eighteenth Century

The number of novels published in France in the eighteenth century increased dramatically when compared to that of the previous century—S. P. Jones has listed no fewer than 946 titles published between 1700 and 1750—but these figures do not indicate by any means a sudden acceptance of the novel as a respectable genre by the critics.[1] For several reasons the novel continued to be steeped in controversy and many ambiguities surfaced during the period. The fact that the novel had no theoretical justification and was not codified by rules suggested that its practitioners could have virtually limitless freedom to experiment.[2]

The resulting diversity and lack of a dominant aesthetic tradition had the effect of exacerbating rather than minimizing the attacks of hostile critics. Novelists in the eighteenth century forged an uneasy alliance with their detractors, capitulating to them at times by engaging in the semantic rituals of such titles as *mémoires, aventures,* or *histoires* or by resorting to the transparent ploy of using the words of fictitious editors or publishers to verify the veracity and moral tenor of their works. The history of the French novel in the eighteenth century and especially during the first decades is extremely complex. The sociological factors that determined the nature of the argument touched upon the very heart of literature as an expression of human culture, for the debate had universal implications that transcended the conventions of a particular age. Questions concerning the true, the plausible, nature, beauty, and the proper subject matter of literature suggested that the influence of the classical doctrine was still pervasive and that the Quarrel of the Ancients and Moderns, which had reached its culmination in the last quarter of the seventeenth century, had not been definitively buried. What was at issue effectively was the concept of realism as it applied to the novel. The ensuing polemic tended to confuse the aesthetic with the moral. As a result, the novel was attacked in the name of taste for being either too implausible or too realistic and was condemned in the name of morality as a corrupting influence because it depicted human vices. One fact is patently clear. The history of the novel in the eighteenth century reveals an effort to regain a lost cause by those who wished to uphold a literature that reflected aristocratic, idealized values, one that resisted the reality of accelerating bourgeois encroachment upon all aspects of French society.

The *Roman* in Its Historical Context

The word *roman,* which first signified a story spoken by the Romans, came to mean, in the twelfth century, texts written in the vulgate or common language. The *romanz* or *romans,* unlike the *chansons de geste* which were written for oral delivery and recited at feasts or fairs, were the forerunners of the modern novel and were read aloud, as opposed to sung, to audiences consisting mainly of women. These were episodic narratives woven around highly idealized themes of love and women. These early *romans* soon evolved into *romans courtois* or medieval romances. The *romans courtois* could be either *romans bretons* or *romans de la table ronde,* thematically linked to tales of King Arthur and his knights or to the Tristan and Iseult legend; there were also *romans d'antiquité,* a group of medieval romances drawn from the writings of ancient Latin authors and *romans d'aventure.* What is significant is that the concept of courtly love that emerged during this period presented a stylized image of human emotions in which passion and virtue were totally incompatible with each other.

The Rise of Bourgeois Literature

As feudal society weakened, a new bourgeois literature emerged which catered more to popular tastes and was directed at a larger public. *Les Quinze Joyes de mariage,* a typical work of this type in the early fifteenth century, marks a radical departure from the idealized image of women and of love in general of the twelfth century. Works of this kind prepared the way for Rabelais who, in the sixteenth century, combined fantasy and extravagance with a vivid representation of the life of all classes of the people. Yet, although there is undoubtedly a strain of popular realism that emerges from Rabelais's comic inventiveness, his very novelty underscores paradoxically the problem of attempting to define the novel along strict structural lines.

At the end of the sixteenth century the *nouvelle* came into greater prominence, distinguishing itself from the *conte,* which dealt with more pleasant subjects and imaginative, implausible works of fantasy, by its more serious or sentimental subjects. The *nouvelle,* moreover, recounted at least plausible events and abandoned the oral tradition that was fundamental to the *conte.* The invention of the printing press undoubtedly played a major role in this development. The rate of illiteracy was still astonishingly high but those who could read were able to find books more readily available. At the same time there seemed to be a move toward the reestablishment of an aristocratic literature that had been temporarily supplanted by the popularity of Rabelais and other writers of similar outlook.

L'Astrée and Its Influence

In the first decades of the seventeenth century one work in particular, d'Urfé's *L'Astrée* (1607–1627), marked a radical shift away from the type of popular literature infused with a special type of realism that Rabelais had embodied. *L'Astrée* bore the mark of the *précieuses,* a group of fashionable women who sought to elevate themselves above others by the elegance of their manners and the purety of their language. *L'Astrée,* a pastoral, sentimental novel, depicted love in an idealized manner. Several romanesque genres were reunited in this very popular work, including the novel of chivalry, the novel of adventure, the tragic history, and the historical novel, but it is the sentimental aspect that dominates and that decrees that feelings be expressed along highly stylized lines.

The ethereal quality of *L'Astrée* was ridiculed by Sorel in *Le Berger extravagant* and in *Francion* and by Furetière in *Le Roman bourgeois.* Reacting to d'Urfé, these authors attempted to create an atmosphere of real life by the depiction of bourgeois or lower-class scenes. Scarron's *Roman comique* represented an important stage in the development of the burlesque novel, another reaction to preciosity.

At the same time, the heroic novels of Mlle de Scudéry marked a transition period between these novels and the literature of French classicism and advanced the cause of aristocratic literature. In her preface to *Ibrahim ou l'illustre bassa* (1641) Mlle de Scudéry spoke about the need to respect verisimilitude, yet this and other heroic novels set in historical frameworks reveal that at this time there was much confusion about the true *(le vrai)* and the plausible *(le vraisemblable).*

History and the Novel

The combining of history with fiction lent an air of verisimilitude to the heroic novel but, as Moses Ratner has pointed out, critics feared that the reader would not be able to distinguish truth from fiction, especially when the characters drawn from antiquity were thought to have been degraded because love was treated as the motivating force behind all their conduct.[3] An ambiguous relationship existed here among the critic, who thought that the reputations of the great would be tarnished by writers who ascribed impure motives to heroes and thus contributed to the process of debunking history; the novelist, who was often more concerned with creating the illusion of truth than basing his narrative on scrupulously researched facts; and the reader, who tended to look upon novels as a form of diversion. The full implications of this link between history and the novel would become apparent in the eighteenth century.

The flowering of the classical doctrine, especially between the years 1660–1685, represented in some respects a return to the aristocratic world view of courtly literature. The summit of this art, influenced by the writings of Descartes with their emphasis on self-knowledge and self-restraint, were the plays of Corneille and Madame de La Fayette's *La Princesse de Clèves*.

The Novel and Classical Doctrines

The concept of *bienséance,* derived from the Latin *decorum,* was at the very heart of French classicism. Internal *bienséance,* which embraced ethical principles, meant conformity to nature, that is, verisimilitude, and this in turn led to a certain type of historical realism. According to this principle, people had to act in conformity with their roles. As an example, kings had to be royal and soldiers had to be brave. The second kind of *bienséance,* external *bienséance,* implied the conformity between art and the public or mores.[4]

Eighteenth-Century Developments

Many eighteenth-century novelists, either because of natural penchant or critical constraint, did not detach themselves totally from the classical aesthetic. Classically oriented authors had distinguished between the true and the plausible, and for them universal truths were more important than historical fact. Lesage, Marivaux, Prévost, and other early eighteenth-century novelists attempted to reconcile this dichotomy and, in English Showalter's view, emphasized the individuality of a character while bringing out fully his type.[5] The novel could evolve in the direction of modern realism only when the historical element was reduced to the status of background and the imaginary circumstances were given more importance. Prévost, Showalter notes, was capable of using a historical framework as a pretext for adventures that clearly strained all credibility.[6]

Vivienne Mylne has noted that one of the fundamental paradoxes in the history of the novel centered about the growing desire of writers to create an illusion of reality and that literary realism, a term used to designate an attempt to represent mores and institutions, in short, the very fabric in which the writer lived, was a nineteenth-century concept.[7] In Philip Stewart's view authors were very much influenced, and therefore constrained, by precepts of classicism at the very moment that they were attempting to broaden the sphere of the novel. The term *histoire,* Stewart points out, was not used to distinguish the historical from the fictitious but rather to describe a work that was not fiction, for fiction was considered antithetical to truth and therefore tainted.[8] On the other hand, the fact that history itself had respectable classical antecedents explains why Prévost and others used historical figures as a backdrop for their fictional narratives.

The Novel and the Passions

Subject matter in the novel in the eighteenth century became more diversified and novelists increasingly chose more contemporary periods as the time frame of their works. The rehabilitation of the passions was another important element that influenced the direction of the novel. In the preceding century La Rochefoucauld was but one voice among many that had warned against the passions: "The passions have an injustice and their own interest which makes them dangerous to follow and one must distrust them even when they appear the most reasonable." The vogue of sensualist philosophy and the influence of the English novelists, especially Samuel Richardson, had the effect of gradually reversing this trend. From being vilified, the passions came to be regarded as an integral part of human nature and their expression was interpreted by many as evidence of the writer's superiority. D'Holbach reflected this vogue when he wrote in the

Système de la Nature in 1771: "To forbid the passions to men is to forbid them to be men."

The popularity of Memoir-Novels during the first decades of the eighteenth century can be explained in part by a philosophical climate that increasingly encouraged the expression of the passions. The first-person narrative form of the Memoir-Novel was an ideal mode for the evocation of the writer's most personal feelings and, at the same time, lent credence to the editor's assurances in his preface that the adventures he had published were true. Speaking of criticism of the French novel during the first half of the eighteenth century, Georges May concludes that the growing trend toward realism in the novel occurred not in spite of the attacks of hostile critics who wished the novel to reflect precepts of classicism, but rather because of such criticism: ". . . the novelists discovered the marvels of realism when their principal aim was to avoid the critics' attacks."[9]

Prévost and the Novel

Henri Coulet states that in the period from 1715 to 1760 critics discussed the novel in terms of *vraisemblance* and moral values, principles of the classical aesthetic that had applied specifically to dramatic literature, because at heart they did not recognize the validity of the novel.[10] The prefaces to Prévost's four major novels suggest not only that he wished to assure his would-be detractors that his narratives were based on facts and were morally edifying but that he also wished to pique the curiosity of a growing reading public for whom events allegedly based on actual occurrences which depict vice and degradation were certain to hold interest.

Prévost's works reveal an important stage in the representation of reality in the novel. English Showalter cites five elements that help to define reality in the novel: chronology, geography, money, names, and the narrator.[11] He shows that Prévost made significant contributions in all these areas to the concept of realism in literature. His treatment of time chronology as subjective, that is, his showing how his narrators' time sense is colored by their emotional state, foreshadows a major theme of nineteenth-century Romanticism and reveals a psychological insight that is rare for the early nineteenth century. Moreover, Prévost is exacting in his treatment of financial matters, and the authenticity of details with respect to money has been verified by Frédéric Deloffre.[12] The same concern for verisimilitude appears in Prévost's use of initials to designate characters, especially in *Manon Lescaut* where other clues leave little doubt about the character's real identity.

It is not in the realm of realism, however, that Prévost's great contribution rests, for his novels evoke a kaleidoscopic vision of the most implausible occurrences. Cleveland falls in love with his daughter, characters are reunited according to coincidences that strain all belief, and time sequences involving geographical movements are not always logical. Patricia Murphy, citing Felix Zimmer's study (*Studien zur Romantechnik des Abbé Prévost,* Coburg: A. Rossteutscher, 1912), lists the kinds of romanesque incidents Prévost borrowed from the heroic-gallant novel that were undoubtedly incorporated more with the intent of pleasing his readers than placating his critics: attacks by robbers or pirates, kidnappings, imprisonments, rescues, freeing of unfortunate beautiful women, disguises, duels, murders and suicides, long sickness and death, supposed deaths, incest, letters intercepted and conversations overheard, dreams that announce future events, mysterious births and inscriptions, ghosts, accidental meetings, religious differences and persecutions, and utopias.[13] Sgard has written that the impossibility of happiness, malaise, the feeling of exile or claustration form the core of Prévost's novels—this "concentration of suffering" which he tries to illustrate and develop.[14]

Prévost's uniqueness is to be found neither in his use of details drawn from eighteenth-century society nor in his dependence on extraordinary events but rather in the very scope of his vision, what Coulet calls a "metaphysical interrogation on nature and on happiness."[15] Prévost's concerns in his novels are those of the philosophes— the nature of human existence, the concept of happiness, human destiny, reason, the passions, morality, and, most significantly, the relationship of these elements. Not surprisingly, Prévost's lengthy meanderings, repetitions, and digressions are stylistically polar to Gustave Flaubert's exquisitely honed statements, for Prévost's life contrasts at every turn with the hermetic existence that Flaubert and Marcel Proust, an even more confirmed recluse, embodied. The richness of Prévost's imagination and the diversity of his characters and situations has led Henri Coulet to decry the tradition that sees Prévost only as the author of *Manon Lescaut.* "He merits," concludes Coulet, "to be considered the equal of Balzac, of Proust or of Dostoyevsky."[16]

Chapter Three

A Picaresque Novel:
Mémoires et aventures
d'un homme de qualité

Man and the World

The ambiguity concerning man's nature and human happiness in the *Mémoires et aventures d'un homme de qualité qui s'est retiré du monde* (Memoirs and adventures of a man of quality who has withdrawn from the world) is foreshadowed by the juxtaposition of three diverse elements in the title: man, the world, and retreat. Thematically the work is structured about a series of dichotomies that embrace such moral, philosophical, and social issues as reason and feeling, authority and individualism, and society and solitude. Suzanne Carroll concludes that Prévost's novels show the limitations of the traditional codes of both religion and gallantry, both of which claim falsely to be universal systems: "The hero vacillates between the two codes, between retreat and life in society, and is never able to find a satisfactory compromise between them or to choose one code over the other."[1]

The first six volumes of the novel bear a special relationship to the part that is invariably published separately under the title *Histoire du Chevalier des Grieux et de Manon Lescaut* (The story of the Chevalier des Grieux and Manon Lescaut). In both sections passion is linked to man's finite nature. The aging Renoncour, who has loved, suffered, and lost, comes to regard his pronouncements against passion as a sacred mission, for he believes that by resurrecting his own experiences as proof of the destructive force of passion, he can spare his charge, the Marquis de Rosemont, from knowing similar anguish. Both Renoncour and des Grieux depict numerous adventures in which passion seems to intensify man's basest desires and is in many cases associated with criminal acts. The two narrators, however, arrive at totally opposite conclusions with respect to the meaning of their adventures.

For Renoncour, passion is a curse, an inalterable force which hovers over man like a sword of Damocles and which had best be avoided. For des Grieux, passion is the supreme good, an entity that transcends all worldly considerations. By its very nature passion cannot endure in society, but in des Grieux's eyes it becomes synonymous with life itself and ultimately resides in a sphere that remains outside the influence of temporal vicissitudes. By virtue of its position in the novel des Grieux's narrative has the effect of "correcting" Renoncour's fundamentally negative view of passion.

Renoncour as Mentor

As moral guide to Rosemont, Renoncour is ostensibly engaged in inculcating in his pupil a disdain for passion and a general acceptance of the principles that will make him a respected *honnête homme,* capable of assuming his place in society as the son of a wealthy nobleman. Renoncour's reactions to the marquis's adventures is conditioned by his own past and he becomes increasingly revealed to the reader, and more significantly to himself, as a romantic who is able to shed neither his inhibitions nor his dreams. In exposing the marquis to the ways of the world Renoncour relives the trauma of his own unhappiness. Like Samuel Beckett's Krapp, Renoncour seems to have been given the luxury of going back in time, but only to discover that the past cannot be relived. In this respect it is Renoncour and not the marquis who comes of age. The marquis's travels to several countries and his involvement with people of oriental background occasion numerous *romanesque* elements, including women disguised as men, duels, abductions, thefts, and premature deaths. These elements and the sheer number of sensational scenes have led Jeanne Monty to conclude that the novel is divided into a series of crises.[2] The dramatic adventures should not obscure, however, the introspective quality of the work which is unified by Renoncour's relentless interrogation on the nature of the passions and their effect on human happiness.

The Role of Sensibility

In the opening pages Renoncour states his reasons for having written these pages. The editor who claimed to have found the work in the course of his travels deemed them worthy of publication because of their very singularity. Jean Sgard has stated that "the truth in

Prévost is not determined by the fabric of the plot or by such and such a character" but rather "from the totality of images and impressions."[3]

The very first paragraph of the body of the text reveals that the narrator, who, we later learn, has detached himself from society, has never detached himself from his own feelings. His writing is directed only at self-edification: "I write of my misfortunes only for my own understanding . . ."[4] Renoncour immediately establishes himself in a long line of Prévostean heroes and heroines whose sensibility distinguishes them from the common run of mankind, for old established values such as an illustrious name and great wealth are not enough to insure happiness "if one's heart is formed in a certain way" (13).

A Pascalian world

The constant human need for diversion that surfaces in these pages recalls Pascal's interpretation of man's restlessness as proof of his inability to confront his condition and his attempt to mask his inevitable destiny. Jeanne Monty has astutely observed that young men in Prévost put their hopes on earthly happiness whereas old men, no longer able to harbor illusions about their chance for lasting worldly reward, turn to thoughts of their salvation because they have exhausted the material realm.[5] Renoncour's movement from the world to retreat is not so much evidence of a religious conversion as it is a sign of his disgust with the world. The vaunted repose, solitude, and opportunity for reflection that he hopes to find in the cloisters represent for him everything that the world is not and with it a shield against the source of his pain. In one sense love in Prévost is a metaphor of life itself, seductive, unpredictable, and capable of causing great suffering because it exists both temporally and spatially and is always in flux. Passion in this novel is an integral part of human nature and constitutes an arena in which man plays out at once his most ennobling and basest instincts. Suffering is at times in Prévost the mark of an exceptional individual but it is more often endemic to existing. The kaleidoscopic series of events, so replete with material objects, seem worlds apart from the sparse tableaux of Samuel Beckett, yet the conclusions of Beckett's Hamm in *Endgame* with respect to the lack of reason and order in the universe might well serve as Renoncour's watchword: "You're on earth, there's no cure for that."

Passion and Free Will

Renoncour, the narrator and mentor to the Marquis de Rosemont, views life as a constant struggle against dissipation and degradation. His strict morality is founded on a belief in original sin. The first crime, he asserts, "rendered all men guilty, weak, and unhappy" (15). The passions, he concludes, originate from man as a result of original sin. What appears to be an ambiguous assignment of responsibility to man for the effects of passion is immediately qualified even further because Renoncour distinguishes between ordinary and extraordinary passions. Whereas concupiscence, which he would place in the first group, is defined as the general penchant men have for women, excessive passion, such as that manifested by his father, is linked to the unsettling caused by the first sin (the Fall), but is different from it. Skirting the issue of assigning ultimate responsibility for extraordinary passions, Renoncour advances a theory of a general Providence which always defies human comprehension: "Providence allows them [the passions] but for reasons which are always worthy of it." Most significantly, love itself is not inherently evil: ". . . love doesn't make us criminal when the object is legitimate" (15). It follows then that if one is not wholly responsible for an excessive passion, he should not be blamed for it; ". . . instead of mistreating a son who finds himself besieged by an excessive passion . . . a father ought to have recourse to gentler methods" (15).

Passion may in and of itself be neutral but the term "besieged," implying an invasion by a foreign body, has unquestionably negative overtones. Renoncour's views on original sin have far-reaching implications. If the passions are an integral part of human nature, they have within them the power to degrade inasmuch as they are linked to our imperfect nature. This duality occurs throughout Prévost. Concupiscence, defined by Renoncour as a natural passion, devoid of reflection (and hence moderation), is but one aspect of passion. Ostensibly man has the free will to make a worthy choice in love, but Providence seems to be lurking in the background, neither benevolently nor malevolently, but rather imparting an unknown final plan. God exists and man exists but God's ways cannot be justified to man. The Prévostean road is a difficult one. The essence of life is mysterious and unknowable. Man can neither explain himself nor can he rely on a higher being for enlightenment. Passion, a manifestation of man's nature, is linked cosmically to the Fall and temporally to all eternity; Renoncour cites his father as an example of one who experienced an extraordinary passion. It is a bridge between generations, a sickness unto death.

The numerous digressions and anecdotes of the secondary characters are integrally related to Renoncour's story, for they reinforce the theme of passion as fatality and unhappiness or, more exactly, the idea that life itself is an incessant struggle against unforeseen dangers and tragedies and that moments of tranquillity are fleeting and exceedingly rare.

Passion and Reason

Human anguish often transcends man's ability to describe it. It is not surprising that Renoncour upholds reason as a critical component of the marquis's education because of his own past feelings which, in their intensity, have defied all his cognitive processes. Attempting to describe his reaction to the death of his young sister Julie, he writes: "It is impossible for me to describe here everything that I felt in my soul and what the excesses of my sorrow were" (24). His father reacted to this death by withdrawing from human society and turning to God because human happiness seemed so futile to him. The religious orders here become synonymous with a kind of psychological death. Although Renoncour's father and others develop in time what appears to be a genuine religious vocation, the initial impulse that took them to the orders remains dominant, the desire to control their environment to such an extent that death becomes the sole event that can intervene and break the pattern of undisturbed calm.

Rosambert's Story

Rosambert's story parallels Renoncour's. He, too, was a solitary figure, a victim of his own impetuousness and man's rapacious behavior. As Rosambert tells his story it becomes clear that human excesses are not limited to the domain of love. Rosambert's own near brush with death causes him to turn his thoughts to God and the concept of Eternity, but once he is out of danger he returns to the world of pleasure. Several conflicts arise in succession, the conflict between his fidelity to Mlle Colman and the religious vows he made when death appeared imminent; the conflict between sexual passion and a woman's honor in the case of the young woman made pregnant by her lover and then abandoned. Finally Rosambert kills the Abbé Levin in a duel.

Rosambert links the beginning of his downfall to his involvement with gambling, which leads to his uncovering card sharps and a duel. Seriously wounded, he views his recovery as a sign of divine intervention: "I would undoubtedly have perished if Heaven had not come to my aid" (32). Since Providence is seen as a mysterious force which intervenes at random in men's lives, Prévost's characters are imbued with an underlying sense of their innocence, a feeling that, not being in control of the major events of their lives, they cannot be held responsible for the outcome. They demonstrate that they know right from wrong, but because of their weaknesses they are the agents of their own misfortunes. The discrepancy between thought and action is a recurrent theme in Prévost.

Passion, as described by Rosambert, means a vague, undefinable disquietude. Hearing that a Parisian widow and her daughter are about to leave Versailles, Rosambert relates: "This news affected me appreciably. In reflecting on the sorrow it caused me I began to feel that my heart was attacked by a serious passion" (35). Odette Kory has observed that ". . . Prévost's intention is to reach the essence of an emotion rather than to study its development."[6]

Passion and Time

Prévost's characters give the impression of living at intense peaks of emotion and experiencing between these highs an ennui that is a kind of nonexistence for them. The very strength of the emotion, once it is nascent, leads to feelings that the individual may find alien because they do not correspond to any previously experienced modes of existence. Feelings in Prévost's novels, notes Georges Poulet, appear as if entirely determined by events. When the event which gave rise to a particular feeling fades, another one takes its place. That is why Poulet describes Prévostean time as "the perpetual substitution of one adventure for another."[7] Prévost's characters, moreover, are often called upon to recount adventures they have already experienced. Typically the feelings associated with the event become more real and hence more significant than the event itself. Passion may lead to dissipation or may constitute a kind of addiction which impairs the rational thought processes. Most often, however, there is no middle ground in Prévost. To avoid feeling entirely, however, is to commit psychological suicide. Repose, tranquillity, solitude are anti-life. As in the case of Beckett's tramps, it is not enough to have lived; one must talk about it. Characters speak about past events not only to revive the feelings associated with the event but also to assess the relationship between feeling and being.

Rosambert is able to experience passion as an ennobling emotion. Declaring his feelings before Mlle de Colman, he adds that his heart was touched by the pregnant condition of the unmarried woman. Drawing on her own experiences, Mlle de Colman implies that women have greater sensibility than men because she had fantasized for years about her perfect lover, imagining qualities that he would possess. Abandoned by her lover, she shows the extremes of passion by killing herself and her unborn child, an act which filled Rosambert with revulsion at the thought of being with any woman in the future. Prévost depicts here the ambivalence caused by passion. Mlle de Colman's initial euphoria gives way to the most intense fury. Unfaithful lovers are treated with the same wrath expressed by Racine's heroines, and feelings of love and hate can be summoned with equal ease by those under the spell of passion. Passion can provide an élan but it can often debilitate and embitter those it affects. A disgust for life, we read, led Renoncour's grandfather to the grave. (51). The ambiguity persists and Prévost never asserts definitively here or in other books of this novel whether it is passion that leads men to extravagant behavior or whether men are susceptible to being overtaken by passion because of their innate instability. The alternative to these states of agitation, which Prévost's characters both seek and deplore, is life behind the physical walls of the religious orders or death.

Passion and Oriental Society

Mlle de Colman had lamented the lot of women who are victimized by rapacious men. Renoncour's adventures in Turkey provide an opportunity for contrasting Western and Oriental mores. Dwelling on the miserable state of his fortune and seeing his past in terms of a succession of losses, Renoncour, nonetheless, avoids the total pessimism of railing out against creation and asks God for help in understanding his troubles. The three books he has on his person reflect various aspects of his future life. *Télémaque* foreshadows his role as mentor to the Marquis de Rosemont and underscores the need for observation and reason in assessing human behavior. La Bruyère's *Caractères,* with its emphasis on man's foibles and immoderate behavior, suggests that man must continually engage in a process of self-examination since the possibility of committing acts of moral evil is always a reality. Finally, Racine's *Tragédies* evokes the theme of love as fatality and signals the intense struggle that exists in the human psyche between rational and affective elements.

Renoncour's foray into the Ottoman Empire exposes him to a society where women ostensibly have much less freedom than in his native France. Affecting a stance as a rational, civilized Westerner, he betrays his own prejudices. He is amazed when the Turk Elid Ibezu treats him with kindness and he is equally unprepared for the old slave Timec's taking the initiative in offering him her affection. Sgard has observed that the harem Prévost describes in this novel is not that of the *Lettres Persanes* where one spies, lies, and kills, but an enchanted universe that the hero crosses.[8]

Renoncour's encounter with Sélima had been prepared by her father, Elid Ibezu. Renoncour soon falls prey to physical desire and his vocabulary reveals the intensity of his passion: ". . . I saw in Sélima one of the most charming persons who has ever been on the earth (69). Most significantly, passion becomes in his eyes an eternal drama which, in its very force, seriously threatens all that lies outside its domain. In time Renoncour discovers that the danger of passion lies in the very ease with which it seduces: "Sélima had made in my heart an impression that would never be effaced from it" (69). The essence of passion in Prévost is contained in this observation. Passion, which attacks suddenly and irrevocably, forever changes those in whom it festers. Fearing that his love may not be returned, Renoncour sees Sélima as the master of his fate and resorts to the language of courtly love: "I am going to die, beautiful Sélima; remember, in learning of my death, that you are the cause of it" (70). One dies in Prévost, however, not because of separation or unrequited love but because passion quickly assumes an autonomy over an individual's life, thereby giving rise to intense conflicts and the expression of jealousy and other violent emotions. Renoncour comes to realize that the fervor of his emotions set in motion a series of violent clashes among the various components of his life—religion, honor, friendship, and love—which tests his ability to maintain a balance between his feelings and his reason.

Renoncour's experiences in Turkey reinforce his awareness that love is unique. Writing of Sélima's brother Amulem, who has fallen in love with Oscine the Sultana, Renoncour notes: "One must have to have loved in order to judge Amulem's feelings at the sight of Oscine" (79). Love in the Orient is no different from love in the West with respect to its potential for violent rage and rebellion. Oscine views with horror her lack of freedom and feels totally degraded when Amulem is congratulated for having made such a beautiful acquisition. When Elid Ibezu dies, Renoncour reflects on the nature of human happiness as he enters the harem with Amulem's permission in order to inform Sélima of her father's death. Physical love, he asserts, is too pleasurable to exist as duration (80). As Proust's Swann, nearly two centuries later, would wish the death of the Vinteuil sonata because the extratemporal feelings it inspired were too intense to be sustained, so must Renoncour seek unconsciously to put an end to what he most fervently seeks.

Passion and the Absurd

The evolution of the Man of Quality's real life has been defined by Jeanne Monty as "this special form of sensibility that is his love for Sélima."[9] Renoncour has married Sélima, who has converted to Christianity. Visiting ancient ruins near Rome, he sees a sight that he believes was inspired by either furious hatred or outraged love—states representing the three Furies, flames, human bones, bodies in states of decomposition (94–95). This view of passion as decay, evocative of Rodin's old courtesan, takes possession of Renoncour's mind and quickly influences his behavior after Sélima's death. At the same time the flame which suddenly shoots from the ashes surrounding the ruin burns Renoncour's hair and frightens him, an occurrence which suggests the tenacity and unpredictability of passion and the almost insurmountable difficulties one has in extirpating it once it has invaded one's body and heart. These ruins, that Renoncour interprets as a sign of the effects of passion, are overwhelmingly negative. Sélima dies soon after. Nothing can justify this premature death. Sgard notes: "Sélima is not the victim of a jealous man or, if there is one, it is the jealous God who doesn't tolerate the happiness of lovers."[10] The link between passion and the absurd becomes clearer with this death. The world is contingent, relative, and operates according to indecipherable laws which seem intent on thwarting individual happiness. Confronting the world, Prévost's characters do not question their own behavior but rather blame an unknown Providence for their misfortunes.

To conclude that happiness is not one's due is to admit that its pursuit is futile and that one must retreat. This is exactly what happens to Renoncour as mentor. Before consciously eradicating all feeling, however, he must first undergo a period of exorcism, his mourning for Sélima. During this year he is neither fully alive nor dead but exists rather on the brink of a death-in-life in which, typical of Prévost, maintaining his sorrow in its most profound form becomes his sole purpose for clinging to life. His placing Sélima's heart in a golden box which he then speaks of as his treasure must be seen not as a maudlin, *romanesque* conceit but rather as an apotheosis of emotion, which ultimately paves the way for him to stifle all emotion. It is obvious that it is above all himself and not Rosemont whom he must convince that his pursuit of a life of contemplation and retreat is morally superior. Discovering, like Caligula, that "men die and they are not happy," he cannot destroy the universe, but rather turns his back on what he perceives to be the cause of his sorrow, thereby abdicating the exercising of his will and his chance for limited, that is human, happiness.

Passion and Retreat

Renoncour believes that the struggle between self-control and self-debasement is incessant but that through an exercise of will the marquis can love in a worthy manner. The intellectualized Corneillean vision of the world that Renoncour attempts to inculcate in his pupil is antithetical to the spontaneous expression of feeling and implies therefore a repression of passion.

Believing that man's innate weaknesses and inability to control an environment shaped by seemingly random laws contribute to a general moral contagion, Renoncour attempts to make a bid for sainthood by imposing a barrier between what he perceives to be a noxious source and himself. Adopting a posture that prefigures Albert Camus's tortured twentieth-century figure, Tarrou, Renoncour functionally withdraws from the world because the world is imperfect, thereby intensifying the absurd and revealing that his efforts to suppress passion have been in vain. Paradoxically Renoncour is never more human than when he fails at his effort to deny his humanity.

Renoncour emphasizes the value of being exposed to directly observed experiences and the need for direct contact with people and events so that his young charge can draw his own conclusions. He insists on the value of his pupil's knowing misery so that he will be sensitive to the plight of needy unfortunates (123). The form of retreat proposed by Renoncour constitutes for him a kind of stability in the midst of perpetual flux: "Our heart is a kind of theater where all the passions play in their turn. It never remains indifferent between good and evil because it is in its nature to always form desires . . . the only remedy is to form solid principles of truth and wisdom for oneself, which can control on occasion the undeliberated penchants of the heart" (130).

Passion and the World

Renoncour teaches his pupil that love is innocent only in theory and that uncontrolled love is a criminal passion which is pitted against honor, fortune, and tranquillity. Soon after this discussion the marquis falls in love with Dona Diana and quickly becomes the victim of her resolve never to love anything with passion. Renoncour feels that he is effecting a compromise between approving of this passion and thwarting it entirely when he advises the marquis to follow Dona Diana's example: "She merits being loved: but love her without passion. Give her your entire esteem. In that way you will spare yourself numerous difficulties and your heart will always be satisfied" (144). Renoncour shows by these words that he has gained only abstract knowledge about human behavior and that he is not yet prepared to deal with the basic human dilemma of acting on his knowledge. The marquis may agree with Renoncour's conclusions about the dangers of passion but in theory only. At the point of accepting Dona Diana's self-imposed conditions of never loving any man with passion, the marquis quickly abandons his stoic mien and laments that he will not be able to survive her loss.

If the marquis demonstrates a breakdown between reason and practice, Dona Diana reveals a gap between feelings and actions. In a posture reminiscent of the Princesse de Clèves at the moment of her ultimate rejection of Nemours, Diana admits that she loves the marquis but wishes nonetheless to renounce the world. She is a female counterpart to Renoncour inasmuch as her unwillingness to settle for limited happiness is itself indicative of the magnitude of her desires. Unable to accept a world that does not conform to her preconceived ideal, she regards herself as a victim of her own sensibility: "I was not born to be happy . . ." (149). Her refusal of the marquis does not imply a positive choice but rather a denial of all emotion and hence a willful accession to a death-in-life, suggested by the words "sacrifice" and "repose." Like Renoncour, she posits an idealized view of human relations in terms of absolute harmony and, sensing inherently the impossibility of fulfilling such an image, she replaces it with an equally absolute one that refuses to make any compromise with human imperfection. The marquis is able to rely on his tenderness and eloquence to save her from a life of emotional suicide. No longer pursuing an unresponsive Dona Diana, the marquis seeks to accommodate his love to society by having society accept it. His words to his father suggest that passion, bearing the mark of Eros, can never be fulfilled in earthly terms. Denis de Rougemont, defining Eros as the object of our supreme desire, notes that "the fulfilment of Love is the denial of any particular terrestrial love, and its Bliss of any particular terrestrial bliss."[11]

Passion and the Human Condition

The marquis's letter to his father underscores the fundamental link between passion and death in Prévost: "My life depends on a word of your hand. I love with more passion than one has ever known" (154). His words to his tutor, moreover, are an expression of passion as a supreme agitation, which undermines self-mastery and defies rational analysis: "I no longer belong to myself" (154). The marquis hopes to convince his mentor of the legitimacy of his passion by recalling Renoncour's own life-threatening sorrow which led him to the secluded orders. Renoncour rejects, however, the marquis's attempts to justify his extreme feelings by distinguishing between the legitimate despair one feels at the loss of a wife and the unjustifiable emotion occasioned by the loss of a mistress. This episode ends, therefore, with a restatement of the dominant view of love in the novel: the passions are a natural reflection of man's finite nature because they reinforce narcissistic impulses, erode his ties with society, and in general give rise to behavior that is more debasing than ennobling.

Through a series of anecdotes and digressions the latter sections of the first six books underscore the link between passion, suffering, loss, and disquietude. Natural goodness does not suffice to guarantee moderate behavior, and Prévost chronicles the clash between individuals on whom passion makes absolute demands and a world that seems to operate according to random laws that thwart individual happiness. Passion, exclusive and absolute, is always potential rather than realization and is in opposition to the ever-changing material world.

The excesses of passion give rise to numerous *romanesque* events, for Prévost's characters are unable to suffer in silence and lash out in rage against those whom they consider responsible for their misfortunes. Often the most horrible fate seems reserved for the most innocent. Brissant, the marquis's schoolmate, scandalized by his criminal behavior that has resulted from his dissipation, relates how, in the course of his conversion, he witnessed the death of a persecuted young girl who, breathing her last, questions the justice of Providence. Dona Diana, having revealed her feelings for Rosemont, is abducted en route to the convent through the plotting of a jealous lover. The marquis kills his rival in a duel and he and Dona Diana are both wounded by the mother of his slain rival. Only when death is imminent is there any respite from the continual unfolding of catastrophic events to which passions give rise.

Significantly, Renoncour is loathe to accept the evidence to which his experiences point, that passion and misfortune are inextricably linked and that men are their own victims. He therefore attributes the consequences of passion to an unknown divine plan: "What use are all human precautions against the immutable disposition of the desires of God: The remedies of art, the cares of love, our wishes, our desires, and our tears, nothing can keep the charming Dona Diana for the marquis" (177).

Conclusion

Feeling that Dona Diana's death is inevitable, the austere Renoncour is moved to tears, not so much tears of sorrow as tears of impotence that reflect man's necessarily passive stance in the face of a destiny over which he lacks ultimate control. Incapable of treating love as a game, Renoncour suffers as do all characters in Prévost who long for lasting harmony that is by definition incompatible with both passion and the world. Concluding that happiness is not to be found in the society of men, Renoncour seeks peace and contentment in religious contemplation, but is unable to divorce himself completely from the world. He therefore attempts to effect a compromise by preaching to the marquis a doctrine of legitimate passion. His dilemma typifies that of the Prévostean hero who is unable to reconcile reason (society, honor, tradition, virtue, religion) with feeling (love) and is consequently consigned to being suspended between worldliness and retreat, finding contentment in neither mode.

Renoncour's experiences reveal to him that the problems of passion, moral evil, and man's state of contingency have neither spatial nor temporal limitations. Although he anticipates a change in fortune, he soon discovers that Portugal is merely Spain with a different name. The story of Dom M.'s unrequited love for Dona Clara becomes all the more unbearable when he learns that she has a burning passion for another man. As in the case of Renoncour and Rosemont, Dom M. discovers that passion overtakes every aspect of his life and, in a moment of perverse generosity, the spares his rival's life because he regards this man as an equally passive agent of Dona Clara's charms: "It depends on her to make me die and to make you live" (203).

The ardor of passion quickly consumes its victim's vitality and results in a state of total emotional dependency. The prolonging of the sorrow occasioned by passion becomes in itself a goal, and self-effacement among Prévost's lovers is no less potent than jealousy and rage. Passion thwarted is no longer characterized by a spontaneous effusion but is rather subject to complex manipulation. Dom M. resolves to nurse his rival back to health so that the "ungrateful Clara" will be obliged to recognize the tenderness he feels for her (205). He later sends his rival, Dom Alonzo, on official business to Brazil for a year in the hope of gaining access to Clara's heart, but the results are disastrous. Passion makes its victims unable to act in accordance with their rational conclusions. Seeing Clara hail her lover as the author of her salvation, Dom M. recognizes that all hope is lost, yet he realizes too that nothing is capable of eradicating his love. For passion in Prévost lies clearly outside the influence of reason, and Renoncour spends years in vain trying to stifle his already-nascent passion by telling himself that passion leads only to anguish and that passion in a man of his age is especially ridiculous.

Violent transports, human inconstancy, and the onslaught of events in which the individual is an innocent victim, all define a universe that seems singularly discordant and that operates from mankind's perspective according to the most random laws. The duality of passion is a mirror of man's condition. Good and evil, happiness and suffering, peace and chaos not only coexist but have meaning only in relation to each other.

Chapter Four

Love as Transcendence:
Histoire du Chevalier des Grieux et de Manon Lescaut

The quantity of critical response to the *Histoire du Chevalier des Grieux et de Manon Lescaut* reflects the complexity of Prévost's most popular work, the seventh volume of the *Mémoires et aventures d'un homme de qualité qui s'est retiré du monde.* Although approaches to this work, published almost exclusively as a separate volume under the title *Manon Lescaut,* have been characterized by a remarkable diversity, most writers have attempted to place des Grieux's narrative in the context of Renoncour's belief in the devastating effects of passion. This in itself has been the source of much controversy.

The apparent simplicity of des Grieux's story, in which a young man of good breeding falls passionately in love with a woman of inferior social station, a *fille de plaisir,* and subsequently knows shame and dishonor in breaking society's laws, has not obscured the multiple resonances which echo on every page. Questions of myth, archetype, and universal cycles of human experience are of critical importance and link the work at once to the Tristan legend, to Pascal's pronouncements on the human heart, and to Rousseau, Freud, Jung, Proust, and other twentieth-century figures. Throughout des Grieux's experiences, however, is the critical question of whether this chevalier is the accursed or elect of passion, whether his story illuminates or repudiates Renoncour's philosophy.

The *Avis*

The *Avis de l'auteur des mémoires d'un homme de qualité* underscores the debate concerning *Manon Lescaut.* Students of the eighteenth century have long known that prefaces to novels are often little more than ploys designed to convince the censor of the author's moral probity. Prévost's *Avis* reflects this concern. We are first told that des Grieux's experiences should be seen as a "terrible example of the force of the passions."[1] The words "force of the passions" suggest that men are incapable of controlling their feelings and should not be held responsible for their actions. Renoncour had repeatedly stated that concupiscence is a natural passion, indifferent to morality, and that men pass with great difficulty to a higher level of feeling, that of virtuous love, which implies rational choice of the object of one's love and self-control. Passion tempered by reason was a possibility in Renoncour's scheme but one which he himself did not feel worthy of testing because, recognizing his own human penchant for excess, he therefore attempted to impose an absolute system of self-negation on himself.

Continuing in the *Avis,* Prévost passes from portraying des Grieux as a victim of natural human impulses to a young man who has chosen his own path of immoderation and self-destruction: "I have to depict a young blind man, who refuses to be happy in order to throw himself willfully into the greatest misfortune; who, with all the qualities of which the most brilliant merit is formed, prefers by choice an obscure and vagabond life to all the advantages of fortune and nature; who foresees his misfortunes, without wishing to avoid them" (363).

The des Grieux who emerges from this description seems to support Renoncour's thesis about the need to recognize the potential evils of passion and detach oneself stoically from the world. In his conclusion to the *Avis,* however, Prévost mitigates somewhat his attack on des Grieux by stating that "all well-born souls" feel that "gentleness and humanity are attractive virtues and are driven by inclination to practice them." These qualities, Prévost goes on to say, often remain submerged when men are called upon to act, which accounts for the fact that there is often a significant deficiency in men's ability to act on their principles (364). Ira Wade has written that the core of Prévost's thought was formed by two questions; How do we think and how do we act? Wade concludes that in his *Avis* Prévost tried to explain the nature of morality and concluded that the individual is free to create his own morality, against all family, all religious, and even all social morality. He thus proclaimed the rights of passion against all social and religious restrictions.[2]

By upholding des Grieux's story as a negative example of how an individual can allow himself to become enslaved to his passions, yet by attributing to des Grieux the naturally virtuous inclinations of any well-bred soul, Prévost skillfully prepared his readers for a narrative that would be linked by contrast to the six previous volumes of the *Mémoires* and that would, at the same time, acknowledge a concern for moral principles. Evidence in favor of des Grieux's case is not long in coming within the first pages of the narrative, for Renoncour, the Man of Quality, reacts favorably on first meeting des Grieux and gives him money. Later, learning of des Grieux's financial condition, Renoncour arranges to have him put up at the Lion d'Or and again gives him money.

The *Histoire du Chevalier des Grieux et de Manon Lescaut* shows the power of the passions but it also counters Renoncour's conclusions. Des Grieux is undoubtedly a soul mate of Renoncour in recognizing this force. But whereas Renoncour decried dormant feelings which he could not suppress, des Grieux lamented the brevity of passion's earthly manifestation. Volume 7 does not intensify the conclusions of the preceding six volumes. It portrays rather an individual who does not subjugate intense feelings but nurtures them. His narrative, woven of the fabric of human weakness, vice, and hypocrisy, stands, nevertheless, as an apotheosis of love in Western literature.

Love: an Essentialist Perspective

Des Grieux's initial meeting with Manon, which defies all rules of causality—des Grieux himself notes that it was by pure chance that he left Amiens on the day Manon was passing in the convoy—becomes the focal point of this entire relationship with the "sovereign of his heart" (369). Henceforth he will be in pursuit of the idealized Manon he creates as a result of their chance encounter. The apprenticeship, which was to have occurred within established social patterns for the son of a wealthy and illustrious family who had just finished his studies, now becomes all-encompassing. Madeleine Morris has observed that Manon is created through the existentialist perspective of des Grieux's eyes and that she always returns to him because he gives her a more seductive image of herself than do any of her other lovers.[3] Similarly, Nancy Miller sees Manon as existing "through the mediation of the illicit couple she forms with a single lover" because she is never able to dramatize herself.[4] Manon is undeniably the creation of des Grieux's regard and exists in the reader's consciousness only because of his vision of her, but whereas existentialism has always implied change and movement, a process of "becoming," the essentialist perspective of des Grieux remains fundamentally static: "She appeared to me to be so charming that . . . I found myself enflamed all of a sudden to the point of transport" (368). Manon will always be for des Grieux an unknown, seductive creature in whom physical charm and beauty are joined with natural goodness. The sight of Manon in effect provides the impetus for the creation of a new des Grieux, one whose entire *raison d'être* will be based on the ecstatic feeling emanating from this first gaze. Such is the intensity of feeling Manon generates that love for des Grieux, comprising more than spiritual or physical entities, becomes synonymous with life itself.

Love as a *Coup de Foudre*

Having drunk Tristan's philtre, des Grieux will henceforth attempt to recapture the idealized situation upon which he was able to impose all the fervor of his latent emotions, a tableau of a Manon whose seductive allure provided him with an extratemporal moment not susceptible to the vicissitudes of everyday reality. Significantly, Manon, distinguished in des Grieux's eyes from the other women in the convoy who had shown a similar penchant for pleasure, exists in a world completely separate from des Grieux's, not only because of obvious class distinctions but also because of the disparity in their worldly experience. The convent to which Manon was to be sent is a punishment for past sins, a death-in-life, whereas the Knights of Malta to which des Grieux aspired represents, as Suzanne Carroll has remarked, his potential for future rewards.[5] The inherent ambiguity of Manon's class situation is in Patrick Brady's view heightened by the fact that both lovers are *déclassé,* Manon in an upward direction, des Grieux in a downward direction, and, in reacting to each other, experience a further social uprooting.[6]

Denis de Rougemont provides the following analysis of the love potion in the Tristan legend:

The love-potion is . . . an *alibi* for passion. It enables each of the two unhappy lovers to say: 'You see, I am not in the least to blame; you see it's more than I can help.' Yet, thanks to this deceptive necessity, everything they do is directed towards the fatal fulfilment they are in love with, and they can approach this fulfilment with a kind of crafty determination and a cunning the more unerring for not being open to moral judgment.[7]

Des Grieux's vision of Manon as the embodiment of all that is beautiful and desirable is, of course, an idealization and must remain untainted from the contingencies of everyday worldly society if it is to be sustained. The scenario for the lovers must necessarily be played out, however, in a Regency setting in which crass materialism influences the course of their lives at every turn. Des Grieux's time with Manon is characterized by repeated cycles where brief periods of happiness, in which the lovers appear to have enough money to live in relative tranquillity, are followed by Manon's betrayal of des Grieux with a series of men (M. de B———, G———, M——— the elder, G———M——— the younger, and the Italian Prince), des Grieux's inevitable despair, and the reunion of the lovers.

Eros and Morality

In order to preserve his vision of a loving, virtuous Manon, despite tangible proof to the contrary, des Grieux replaces the world's standard of judgment by what Robert De Rycke has called the standard of Eros.[8] The tension between these two standards is perpetuated precisely because the lovers are constantly in society. Des Grieux's essentialist view of Manon is extended to include his own behavior as well as hers. He can substitute the standard of Eros for that of society by insisting not only on Manon's uniqueness but also on his own extraordinary capacity to feel. The lovers then can be judged not in terms of what they do but in terms of what des Grieux believes they *are,* two star-crossed individuals whose forays into deceit, gambling, thievery, and even murder cannot obscure what he perceives to be their basically noble intentions. There is a fundamental disparity on the moral plane between what Prévost's characters do and what they say, notes Vivienne Mylne.[9] Similarly, Raymond Picard cites examples of how des Grieux, under the spell of Eros, resorts to casuistry, even after having killed the guard at Saint-Lazare, explaining that he neither asked for the loaded pistol nor intended to commit murder.[10]

Reality in the form of psychological barriers also contributes directly to the frenzied movement that marks their cycles of happiness, betrayal, anguish, and reunion, for while des Grieux's concept of love demands absolute fidelity, Manon, in Alan Singerman's view, condemned to a demimonde exile by a society that tolerates her only as a *fille de plaisir,* can offer des Grieux only a fidelity of the heart and must relegate him to the rôle of *greluchon* (fancy lover) in conformity to her own place in society.[11]

The language of the narrative is infused with repeated references to the power of passion and the singularity of des Grieux's feelings. Jeanne Monty, who generally views des Grieux as a weak and thoroughly unattractive person, concludes that, by the example of the chevalier, Prévost wished to show that an individual must have the will to control his passions through reason, thereby controlling to some extent his own destiny,[12] since Manon, or more precisely, the thought of being loved by Manon, becomes for des Grieux the only way of achieving happiness. One thinks particularly of his exchanges with Tiberge, his loyal friend who represents the socially acceptable values of reason and honor. Here the possibility of more immediate tangible rewards is contrasted favorably with the hope of achieving eternal life. It seems more accurate to say, therefore, that des Grieux regards himself as the elect of passion while Manon is alive and is prepared to suffer by virtue of this election. He never abandons the idea that life without her would bring inconceivable anguish even though he is very much aware that the pursuit of Manon occasions great suffering. Des Grieux does violate society's laws and attributes his behavior to the force of his love. To the extent, however, that his passion for Manon becomes identifiable in his mind with life itself, and therefore the ultimate good, his will is not so much paralyzed with respect to making choices between two modes of existence as it is influenced by the belief that there is no choice to be made. Having willed the way of passion, he then permits himself everything on behalf of his feelings.

Toward the end of his arduous pursuit of Manon, des Grieux explains his decision to accompany her to Louisiana by stating that he has to yield to the rigors of his fate. Long before his idol's banishment to the New World he had discovered that she was able to elicit conflicting feelings in him: "The more I knew her, the more I discovered new pleasing qualities in her. Her mind, her heart, her sweetness, and her beauty formed so strong and charming a chain that I would have disposed of all my happiness to never leave it. Terrible change! What creates my despair could contribute to my happiness" (370).

As a result of his inability to possess completely another individual

(in Manon's case the physical separations only underscore the psychological distance created by Manon's need for money), des Grieux
makes the link between passion and suffering soon after his transfor-
mation, and his passion therefore comes to embody the phenomenon
of what Rougemont calls "unhappy mutual love." Rougemont explains: "Passion means suffering, something undergone, the mastery
of fate over a free and responsible person. To love love more than the
object of love, to love passion for its own sake, has been to love to
suffer and to court suffering all the way from Augustine's *amabam
amare* down to modern romanticism."[13]

Des Grieux's ability to express emotion becomes synonymous in his
mind with the purity of his motives. Thus, seeing Manon shed unex-
plained tears at dinner, he recounts: "I begged her, with all the zeal-
ousness of love to tell me the cause of her tears; I shed some myself
in drying hers; I was more dead than alive" (372). When he hears of
Manon's escapades with M. de B . . ., he reveals that his powers of
reason are no match for his emotions: ". . . how would I have es-
teemed the most fickle and the most perfidious of all creatures? But
her image, the charming traits that I bore in the depths of my heart
still remained there" (374).

The various threads in the narrative are linked by des Grieux's
growing belief that the human heart is impenetrable. Yet it is not
the accumulation of heartbreaking events that confers a tragic tone on
his story but rather his unwillingness to sacrifice the true life which
he believes comes only from passion. Passion and suffering become
inextricably linked in his mind. "I was born for brief joys and long
suffering" (389). His suffering is at times expressed as stifled feeling.
Thus, when he hears that an Italian prince is infatuated with Manon:
"I couldn't make it a crime for Manon to be loved" (408). He states
shortly after: "This charming creature was so absolutely the mistress
of my soul that I did not have a single feeling that was not esteem
and love" (411). His suppression of jealousy reveals the degree of his
anguish: "Far from making it a crime for Manon to have pleased the
younger G . . . M . . . I was delighted with the effects of her charms
and I applauded myself for being loved by a girl whom everyone
found likable" (411).

The morality of Eros directly influences the rhythm of the narrative. Actions and feelings are juxtaposed. Georges Poulet finds that
each episode ends with a totally unexpected catastrophe and is fol-

lowed by the beginning of another so that one is left with an accumulation of completely separated fragments. Poulet's concept of the "instant-passage" in Prévost seems particularly applicable to the intensity of emotion des Grieux knows as a result of his having been intoxicated by Manon: "It is the instant in which extremes meet . . . it is a passage from the greatest joy to the greatest sorrow and from the greatest sorrow to the greatest joy. . . ."[14]

Passion, Sensibility, and Self-Knowledge

In a rare moment when des Grieux looks back at his past life (Lescaut has just informed him of his most recent escapades with his sister), he admits how far his recent adventures have carried him from the innocence he knew while under his father's authority. He insists, however, that love itself is free of evil and corruption and blames his misery on a force that he can neither understand nor control. Significantly, he affirms, by implication, his own natural goodness and remains emotionally attached, while decrying the vicissitudes of past fortune, to a happier future with Manon: "It was at this moment when honor and virtue made me still feel the points of remorse and when I turned my eyes . . . toward my father's house . . . By what fatality, I said, have I become so criminal? Love is an innocent passion; how has it changed for me into a source of miseries and disorders?" (388).

The nineteenth century saw the rise of a literary phenomenon known as Bovarysme, the tendency to see the world as the world is not, the attempt to deny present banal reality by reviving a past infused with the afterglow of created reminiscence or envisaging a future marked by exotic beauty. Des Grieux's dreams, inspired by the vision of an idealized Manon are linked to the intense emotional states associated with his beloved whereby feelings of joy, sorrow, fear, and bewilderment follow one another in rapid succession. Whereas des Grieux attempts to define happiness in terms of a concrete, seemingly inviolable state—living in tranquillity with Manon—Flaubert's Emma Bovary recognizes in her most revealingly introspective moment that she had never been happy, that her hopes centered about untested dreams. Des Grieux's dreams involve extension of self—his most sacred command from Eros is to do everything he can for Manon. Emma's are unspecified but have the common effect of tainting all that she touches.

The Sense of an Election

Prévost poses the tension in des Grieux's life in terms of two separate existences, a real one comprised of manipulation, deceit, and monetary concerns, the other a fantasized, exotic existence far removed from the tangible concerns of everyday life and characterized by the harmonious display of intense emotions, a transcendence of hearts among lovers. Des Grieux's imagined ideal life with Manon is, of course, repeatedly assailed by the intrusion of material reality. The pressures of everyday society, which involve both Manon and des Grieux in elaborate schemes to procure money, serve only to attach des Grieux with greater urgency to his dream of a life with Manon lived out in complete tranquillity. To abandon the pursuit of Manon would destroy what has now totally encompassed and defined his identity, an existence based on feeling, wherein, he believes, lies the proof of his superiority. [15]

Des Grieux exults in his superior sensibility and sees in this quality the ability to detach himself from the crass acts he commits: "The common run of men are sensitive to only five or six passions . . . But persons of a more noble character can be moved in a thousand different ways" (391–392). He is able to disallow his "criminal" acts because he is convinced that love is an innocent passion and that one's ability to feel is a sign of superior character. Implicit here is the notion that, since his extraordinary sensibility sets him apart from the crowd, he is destined to be misunderstood by his detractors. It follows, too, that those who possess the capacity to know such emotional heights cannot be otherwise and should not be attracted by ordinary mortals. If passion is irresistible, des Grieux's story should elicit sympathy, and perhaps even pity, but not blame.

Throughout his *Confessions* Jean-Jacques Rousseau asserted that his consummate individuality justified his existence. Rousseau believed that knowledge of others, the penetration of another's being, is rarely achieved because of the complexity of the emotions that each individual harbors within himself. Rousseau undeniably wished to exonerate himself of blame for blatant acts of immorality he had committed. His appeal to a universal relativism is already hinted at in the tone of des Grieux's narrative. For Prévost's hero is also struck by the discrepancy between appearance and reality and, for all his penchant for analysis, reveals throughout his narrative that he knows himself as little as he knows Manon.

In *Manon Lescaut* Prévost takes the epistomological questions of the seventeenth century with respect to how man acquires knowledge and what man is capable of knowing and focuses on passion as an impenetrable force that defies conventional laws. The sense of the absurd that permeates this novel results in part from the acceleration of external events that impede the lovers' bliss but most of all from the Tiberges and paternal figures who claim to possess a higher order of understanding than des Grieux of a world whose fundamental mysteries they minimize or even deny. They do not perceive what Deloffre calls the "great difficulty in judging others' actions morally because one is never completely informed of the real intention that gives them their meaning."[16]

In one sense the novel examines the individual's struggle against the curse attached to love since love is excluded from society. Des Grieux's father condescendingly promises his son to find for him a girl who resembles Manon, thus revealing how little he understands the nature of his son's feelings. Just before Manon is about to be deported to America des Grieux implores his father to reverse his decision. One glimpse of Manon, he cries out, will make his father see immediately the injustice of G . . . M . . .'s calumny: "You would have sided with her . . . You would have had compassion for her and for me" (428). But the father chooses not to cast his eyes on his son's seductress, and so the distance between reason and feeling remains, never to be bridged.

Passion and Dependence

Many critics have commented on des Grieux's egoism, noting that, despite his fraudulent acts and skirmishes with the law, he occupies a much more secure social position than Manon and readily turns to Tiberge for financial assistance or has the opportunity to return to his father's house. Lionel Gossman sees in Manon's leaving des Grieux for G . . . M . . . the younger, evidence of her selfishness in contradiction to des Grieux's belief that "she ceases to be herself only when she is in need."[17] For, as Gossman points out, Manon is in no immediate threat of poverty at this point in the narrative. Monty views des Grieux as an example of what Rousseau would call "l'homme naturel," preoccupied with the satisfaction of his own desires and instinctively doing good to others if their interests do not conflict with his.[18] In truth, however, Manon, restricted by her past actions to living on the fringes of society, actually is much freer than des Grieux because her value system, unlike his, does not demand absolute physical fidelity. In Gossman's words, "Manon upholds free love, not as libertinage, but simply loving freely without desire to master or possess."[19] Frédéric Deloffre speaks of des Grieux's passion as exclusive and Manon's love as an affectionate and tender taste, and concludes by implication that the novel represents the antithesis to the Corneillean concept of love: "The divorce between love and esteem is consummated here."[20] In fact, des Grieux passes beyond esteem in his sentiments toward Manon. Manon is increasingly spiritualized by his regard, but the element of physical passion is retained. In effect, the elements of courtly love coexist with the passion of the boudoir. These conflicting qualities, all revealed through des Grieux's eyes, make Manon a legendary *femme fatale,* an elusive, alluring creature, the embodiment of the eternally feminine.

The scene in which Manon, cavorting with G . . . M . . . the younger, finds herself unable to meet des Grieux at the Comédie and sends a replacement reveals the typically addictive nature of passion. Des Grieux finds Manon's letter insulting and cruel, lashes out against all women, and threatens to abandon Manon forever. The violent mortal jealousy which was breaking his heart was disguised in a "mournful and somber tranquillity." Apparent calm, however, immediately gives way to "a terrible state of fury" as he realizes that he has been the dupe of love (413–14). This second phase is soon followed by a period of profound sadness and agitation wherein, in a state of uncontrolled emotion, he calls for Manon, then repels her replacement. Seemingly purged after having experienced a series of tumultuous emotions, he is able to analyze his situation with surprising lucidity: "I knew Manon: Why torture myself because of a misfortune that I should have foreseen?" (415) When he sees Manon shortly after, his emotion similarly runs the gamut from tenderness to anger and finally to complete submission and dependence on her desires: ". . . I would have had to lose all feeling of humanity to become hardened against so many charms . . . I took her between my arms. I gave her a thousand tender kisses. I asked her forgiveness for my fit of anger. I confessed that I was a brute and didn't deserve the happiness of being loved by a girl like her" (417).

Passion and the Absurd

In his analysis of *Manon Lescaut* Ira Wade speaks of a discord in the novel between the rights of nature and the rights of reason, even between grace and happiness.[21] This latter conflict is exemplified in the exchange between des Grieux and Tiberge during des Grieux's internment at Saint-Lazare: Des Grieux asks his friend: "Will you say, as the mystics do, that what torments the body is a happiness for the soul? . . . I love Manon; I strive to live happy and tranquil near her through a thousand sorrows. The path where I walk is unhappy, but the hope of arriving at my end still infuses it with sweetness . . . The happiness I hope for is near and the other is far . . ." (395). The Pascalian division between mind and body is dramatized here. There is no common ground between des Grieux's sensible existence and Tiberge's reasonable existence. Pascal's famous pronouncement—"The heart has its reasons that reason knowest not"—is reexamined in favor of des Grieux. Paradoxically, des Grieux, who claims to possess a degree of sensibility that distinguishes him from the multitude, defends his behavior by citing the widespread immorality of society and thus tries to persuade those who would condemn him that he is no different from other men.

Wade also speaks of Prévost's having "taken over Racine's theme of love . . . placed it in a setting which was dominated by a blind fatality nurtured by the passions, by social obstacles and by the inherent absurdity of life."[22] The psychological distance that separates the lovers because of their different social status has already been discussed. External events such as fire and thefts are other sources of mental anguish to des Grieux because the resulting financial losses hasten Manon's search for lovers who will be able to keep her in a more luxurious style. The novel is permeated most consistently, however, by a sense of the fundamental absurdity of life, by a divorce between desire and reality, between expectation and result, between appearing and being. Confronted by old G . . . M . . . whom he has attempted to swindle, des Grieux reflects bitterly on the unavoidable prison sentence he will receive and especially on Manon's fate: "What fate for so charming a creature . . . Why were we not born, one and the other, with qualities conforming to our misery? We received intelligence, taste, feelings. Alas! what sad use we make of them, while so many base souls worthy of our fate enjoy all the favors of fortune!" (423).

The link between passion, suffering, and the question of human happiness is underscored in these words. Passion may bring suffering, yet the promise of an elusive happiness, never concretized, is in des Grieux's eyes infinitely preferable to Tiberge's reasonable existence. Feeling is for des Grieux indistinguishable from living and allows him not only to gain an apprenticeship into life but also adds a qualitative stamp to existence: "Love is a good teacher . . ." (407). Happiness, conceived always in terms of expectation, clashes with even the remotest hint of what it purports to seek—fulfilment, and the cycle of the absurd is perpetuated unto death.

The New World and Manon's Death

The physical banishment of the lovers to a far-off continent emphasizes the psychological exile they had experienced in European society. Thoughts of life with Manon in an unknown exotic region change the character of des Grieux's dreams. Having heeded the ultimate demands of Eros and followed Manon to the ends of the earth, he harbors no illusions about the possibility of living with her in sheer ecstasy, indifferent to material needs. The substance of his passion—to love and be loved by Manon—would have led him to reply affirmatively to the question Manon had posed in one of her letters— "Can one be happy without bread?"—but the des Grieux who envisages life in the New World with his idol can no longer minimize the importance of life's daily exigencies (432). He is far from able, however, to divest himself completely of his dreams of idyllic happiness with Manon. Thoughts of an unknown land engender another illusion, a society in sharp contrast to that which he had left, one inhabited only by savages who, neither greedy nor bound to constraining codes of honor and living according to the laws of nature, would allow him to share with Manon a simple mode of life. This assumption proves to be patently false in the course of time and precipitates the events that result in Manon's death.

Sensing the nature of the sacrifice that des Grieux has made for her in his willingness to share her exile (although typically to the last moment before his departure des Grieux seeks money from Tiberge), Manon declares her complete devotion to her lover and tells him that he is loved the most tenderly of any man in the world. Des Grieux's created ideal image of Manon had always been in conflict with reality. His response to her words conveys his fears of realizing his hitherto unattainable ideal—an adoring Manon, liberated from the shackles of an oppressive society, apparently lies within his grasp: ". . . Be careful, be careful, my dear Manon. I do not have enough strength to withstand such vivid signs of your affection. I am not accustomed to these excesses of joy" (434). For des Grieux the tragedy of loving becomes for an instant the tragedy of being loved. Having been deprived of her individuality within the social order as a provider of pleasure, an existence within what Joseph Donohue calls the *"superflu si nécessaire* of urban civilization,"[23] Manon is now able to devote herself completely to des Grieux. The apparent realization of the dream, however, is antithetical to the intense feelings engendered by passion, and des Grieux, as Gossman writes, "still tries to define an essence of Manon," a desire undoubtedly intensified by his disillusionment with the behavior of men in the society he left behind.[24] "Manon," he states, "was never an irreligious girl" (435). Believing that happiness with Manon must extend beyond their intimate existence and be recognized by the community of men, des Grieux proposes that they get married. His revelation that Manon had never been previously married prepares the way for Synnelet, the governor's nephew, to declare his passion, an act which Mylne cites as an example of Manon's still exerting her fatal charm in the New World.[25] Perhaps more accurately it is another example of des Grieux's having misjudged human nature, a final proof that love and society cannot be reconciled. This time there is no encouragement from Manon. Her love for des Grieux has become absolute, in Alan Singerman's view, because he has chosen to share her exile.[26] Des Grieux's ultimate disinclination to live a modest life with Manon outside the bonds of marriage is significant. Living a simple existence with Manon signals the death of the dream, for under these conditions her image as the unattainable, mysterious creature whose purity transcended earthly concerns, must necessarily erode.

By her death Manon becomes the idea of her that des Grieux always wanted. The words designated to convey the moment—"I lost her"—are bitterly ironic in the sense that by her death des Grieux at last finds her, complete and inalterable, the Manon whose essence he had frozen at their first meeting and that had become inseparable from existence itself. Deloffre notes that the dead Manon is admired by des Grieux like a statue and loses her human dimension.[27] In one sense she never had been human for des Grieux. The physical Manon, the *catin* whom he and numerous other men enjoyed taking to bed (des Grieux repeatedly speaks of her beauty and charm without ever providing specific details of her appearance) had been consistently overshadowed by the image of Manon as idea. Manon dead becomes the embodiment of purity, a deified figure whose story, like that of Christ, the Man-God who similarly roamed the earth, assumes its meaning only in her sacrifice (her death). For the earthly character has now become the mythical one and des Grieux is at last able to possess the essential Manon—eternal, unchanging, and beyond subjective time.

Des Grieux as Character and Narrator

The des Grieux who returns to the society of men some time after Manon's death praises Heaven, which "after having punished me with so much severity had the design to render my misfortune and punishment useful" (440). He is not the "sadder but wiser" man who, having been condemned by society for a love deemed unworthy of him and having committed criminal acts in the name of this love, returns to "principles worthy of his birth and education" and attempts to forget his past with Manon (440). Jean-Luc Jaccard has pointed out that, having reached the state of complete disillusionment with society, des Grieux realizes that happiness is no longer possible in the society of men but comes to grasp a happiness that can no longer be destroyed, the untouched state of purity made possible by Manon's death.[28] Jaccard views des Grieux both as a character in the story (the "time of adventure") and a narrator (the "time of narration") whose story is therefore recounted on two levels, how it was lived in the past and how it is felt in the present.[29] Because the story is told from the perspective of Manon's death, the end is the beginning and the emphasis is therefore not on what happened (the factual level) but how it came to happen (the significant level). Des Grieux as narrator is able to fix Manon forever in his mind as an innocent victim of society. His essentialist view of her, which conflicted with the reality of facts while Manon was alive, can now be preserved intact and his quest for a "paradise lost," similar to that which he knew when he first met Manon, is now realized. Manon dead becomes spiritualized in des Grieux's eyes. The victory of love is now definitive, made possible by eternal absence. Manon spiritualized, as opposed to the earthly, carnal Manon, cannot be tainted by reality.

As des Grieux narrates the story of his life with Manon and her death, he becomes involved also in a quest for his own identity. Having ascertained the power of Eros, he accedes to its demands and makes little effort to resist it. In the course of his pilgrim's progress his self-blame is often a thinly disguised attempt at self-exoneration in view of what he feels is the irresistible pull of passion and his own uncommon capacity to feel. His descent from lofty aristocratic heights into what Manfred Kusch describes as "the everyday world of men and women of mediocre virtue" and his apparent return to the world of his father do not negate the fact that, just as Manon was the creation of his youthful ardor and desire to spiritualize and render eternal that which is contingent, so, too, does des Grieux live only in Manon.[30] Thus he remains as fixed in time as Manon. *"Il n'y a pas d'amour heureux"* ("There is no happy love"), wrote Louis Aragon, echoing the indissoluble element that has linked passion throughout the centuries. Lasting, meaningful happiness is indeed chimerical in earthly terms in Prévost. But for the individual who is able to draw on his own resources the human adventure can involve a process of spiritualization. Des Grieux's story is not a "terrible example of the force of the passions" but a chronicle of man's need to ennoble that which is banal, flawed, and mortal, to create an essence of purity that is beyond temporal and spatial change. Des Grieux is a definitive rejoinder to Renoncour and his story is a tale of striking beauty.

Chapter Five

Prévost's Melancholy Philosopher: *Le Philosophe anglais*

Cleveland and the World

Le Philosophe anglais, ou histoire de Monsieur Cleveland (The English philosopher, or History of Monsieur Cleveland), Prévost's most ambitious work, is extremely difficult to categorize. It appears to be predominantly a work of apprenticeship in which the hero, armed with untested theories, is forced to judge the efficacy of his beliefs when he is thrust into contact with men and the world. Richard Desroches believes that *Cleveland* is an exemplary eighteenth-century novel in its reliance on an unending succession of episodes marked by incredible adventures.[1] It is, at the same time, more circular than linear, for the Cleveland who adheres to an absolute concept of happiness discovers that neither philosophy nor feeling nor society nor religion alone can provide the inner peace he seeks so desperately. Cleveland's adventures and those of other characters bring them into contact with utopic societies and thus show from another perspective that the need to dominate is a major trait of human nature and that instability, restlessness, and contradiction know no geographical or temporal boundaries. Cleveland, the tired traveler, returns to the self as the surest basis for knowledge and, like many of Voltaire's heroes, posits a negative truth, the limits of reason. The elaborate labyrinth of his adventures leads, then, not to a definitive conclusion but rather to skepticism and a definition of man in relative terms.

Cleveland is an open-ended novel precisely because its protagonist comes to proclaim the fragility of human happiness and the seemingly insurmountable gap between desire and reality. The universality of his concerns links him to the modern absurdist hero who is adrift in a universe he can neither explain nor control. Here, as in other works of Prévost, love may bring suffering, philosophy may prove to be inadequate in the face of personal disasters, an individual may seek friendship but is often the victim of worldly ambition, religion may leave too many questions unanswered, yet the Hobbesian universe of unrestrained passion and self-seeking is but one side of the picture. Voltaire rejected the thoroughgoing pessimism of the *Leviathan* on the grounds that, if all were evil, man would have destroyed himself long ago. For as Ira Wade has observed, critics of the eighteenth century have recognized that "whatever trait has been emphasized as characteristic practically always must be complemented by its opposite."[2]

Cleveland, *une âme sensible*

Cleveland's explanation of his reasons for writing his memoirs establishes him among the ranks of the elite group of the sensitive heart, one who has been marked by destiny to experience powerful emotions and who derives great satisfaction in being able to share his misfortune with others in a *transparence de coeurs* reminiscent of Rousseau, a fellowship with equally sensitive souls. By suggesting that intense feelings of happiness and sadness remain undifferentiated for those capable of great passions which enter the realm of pure feeling, Prévost already foreshadows what will become a major leitmotiv of this novel, the identification of feeling with existence itself: "All unfortunate men know too well that the sweetest consolation of a great sorrow is to have the freedom to complain about it and to appear affected. The heart of an unfortunate one is as much idolatrous of its sadness as a happy and satisfied heart is of its pleasure."[3] In this respect Cleveland takes his place alongside des Grieux and other Prévostean heroes who, in knowing states of extreme passion, attain a level of existence beyond the reach of ordinary man.

Rumney-Hole: Cleveland's Earliest Education

Elizabeth Cleveland's self-imposed exile from society is cloaked in ambiguity. The victim of lust and worldly ambition, Elizabeth suffered as a woman for not having behaved according to acceptable standards, for her social persona was too strongly influenced by her inner feelings: "The world forgives a woman certain weaknesses which appear ennobled by their cause . . . But . . . all women who forget their duty by the transport of a blind passion are generally viewed with suspicion" (18).

In educating her son, Elizabeth sought primarily to inculcate moral principles. Acknowledging man's duality, his heart and mind, she stressed nonetheless that a balance between the two required constant vigilance. Twice the victim of men's ambition, first of Charles I, then of Cromwell, Elizabeth teaches a philosophy derived from the conflict she herself has experienced, between reason and the passions that destroyed her peace of mind: ". . . she knew that weaknesses and needs of the body are continually opposed to the tranquillity that contributes to the happiness of the soul; that philosophy, in calming the passions, does not make one insensitive to the necessities of nature . . . " (21).

The equilibrium between heart and mind, on the one hand, and the bodily passions, on the other, exists as a theoretical ideal only for Elizabeth Cleveland inasmuch as her self-imposed exile into the tomb-like existence of Rumney-Hole suggests her defeat at the hands of the world. Her stoicism, resulting from a deep-seated distrust and fear of society, will have a lasting effect on her son who himself will come to proclaim in time his own "invincible horror of life." Cromwell, Cleveland's father, moreover, is a constant reminder of the corruption of men and their institutions. Like Mme de Chartres, Elizabeth presents a confused and contradictory message by upholding the possibility of man's exercising his natural goodness and innocence, yet proclaiming the rampant evil of men in society and further stipulating the individual's need for constant self-observation and self-control. The strength of character she so admires and that forms the basis of the moral philosophy she teaches her son is extracted from books, and the examples of great virtuous men of the past only heightens Cleveland's awareness of the injustices perpetrated by those living in the present. Believing that human history is a record of horrors and excesses, Elizabeth is nonetheless confident that her son, raised in isolation, will be able to maintain the control over his passions that alone can insure the tranquillity of his soul:

You are young, you have been brought up in the repose of a profound solitude: your heart has never felt a violent passion, and your brain has never received any traces that were able to make too strong an impression on your soul. Thus, the principles of natural innocence still exist in you in their integrity . . . Add the care that I have taken to inspire in you early the soundest ideas of virtue and to fortify nature in this way by the aid of education. If happiness and peace were difficult to acquire in a heart such as yours, one would then have to consider them as dreams and impossibilities (34).

It is in Mme Riding's cave, seeking refuge with his mother, that Cleveland reveals how thoroughly he has accepted his mother's philosophy and how ill prepared he is consequently to assume a role in adult philosophy: "Imagine men without passions on Earth, you would have a society of happy persons . . . The very obscurity of our domicile can aid the tranquillity of our soul" (33).

For des Grieux, raised to assume a conventional role in society, the experience of passion occasions a feeling of intense conflict with the world of his father, as he both curses and nurtures his passion. A love story is at the center of *Cleveland,* too, but in this case the lover is drawn increasingly to accepting society's norms, and his sentiments for Fanny, influenced by principles of Corneillean moderation, lead him to feel esteem as well as physical attraction for Axminster's daughter. Unlike Manon, Fanny is no love goddess but rather Cleveland's wife and the mother of his children, yet des Grieux and Cleveland are kindred souls, both of whom come to proclaim what Roddier describes as "the powerlessness of natural philosophy to cure the sufferings of the heart."[4]

The Nature of Passion

Philip Stewart has convincingly shown that feeling exists before knowing for Cleveland and that nature's voice (adolescent sexual arousal) is ambiguous precisely because it is experienced before it is understood.[5] The fifteen-year-old Cleveland thinks about Mylord Axminster's daughter Fanny in terms of a "feu secret" in his veins, which he "felt before knowing its nature." Because Cleveland discovers in himself the symptoms of love without knowing what it is, Stewart concludes that the text challenges the belief that love is a natural inspiration by linking it rather with knowledge. Cleveland's fundamental awareness of love comes from books and the first signs of his feelings for Fanny are depicted in Corneillean terms. His is no sudden violent *coup de foudre* but rather an intellectual process that forces him to feel shame at sensing the disparity between his social position and Fanny's. His encounter with Fanny elicits in him a desire to uphold an untenable ideal, the absolute balance between feeling and reason which his mother proclaimed was indispensable to his happiness. Just as des Grieux pursues an idealized vision of a Manon who transcends worldly vicissitudes, so does Cleveland react with increasing dismay as his mother's philosophy is undermined by men and events. His coming of age is in large part a function of his growing realization that his mother's code is of little practical application. His shifting fortunes and attitudes involve not only geographical changes but, more significantly, an attempt to reconcile the theoretical ideal of happiness and peace with reality. Carroll sees Prévost examining in *Cleveland* the claim that "philosophy is a universal system" which "transcends the limitations of religion and gallantry."[6] When love as a dominant mode of existence does not fulfill its promise of inner peace, Cleveland turns to study, philosophy, friendship, and ultimately to religion as a means of finding the happiness that he firmly believes is his right.

Cleveland's Quest for Happiness

Obsessed with the importance of observing his feelings, a legacy from his mother, Cleveland enters the world with a degree of self-consciousness that convinces him of his uniqueness and his capacity to experience exceptional feelings. He rails against misfortune because he is repeatedly confronted with scenarios that are stylistically incompatible with his preconceived image. Des Grieux, raised in a world of assumed essences, greatly accelerates the tempo of his existence when, after meeting Manon, he attempts to direct the course of his destiny. His dreams of living with Manon in seclusion from society clash with the intense energy generated by his passion, and the image of Manon that he fixes in his mind—that of a victim whose goodness contrasts with the baseness of her tormentors—can paradoxically be sustained only in a social setting. Cleveland, in contrast, approaches his life in society from the perspective of the stasis he knew at Rumney-Hole and the various "stages" of his existence in which he turns to a dominant mode, be it love, philosophy, friendship, or religion, to bring him happiness, reveal his desire to stop the flow of time and hence to eliminate all chance. Predictably then, since Cleveland bases his frame of reference on abstractions, he accepts the premise that life in society is both natural and desirable but judges himself and his environment in terms of his idealized "norm." His intense search for an unrealized happiness evokes Pascalian malaise. Whereas for Pascal man's need to lose himself in diversion was indicative of a spiritual

unrest that could be cured only if faith were professed in the God of
the Roman Catholic Church, Cleveland's quest to reach out and extend himself beyond the immediate and finite brings him back to his
own image. Rita Winandy sees in Cleveland's unrest a resemblance
to John Locke's ideas in *An Essay Concerning Human Understanding:*
uneasiness, desire, and the longing for an unidentified and absent
good.[7]

Although Cleveland remains attached to his mother's stoical vision
of the world ("I wished to become happy through love . . . I had two
goals . . . What was the other? It was to work incessantly to make
me wise with the help of my study and my reflections . . ."), his
principles of self-control and moderation are no match for his emotions (85). When Fanny confesses her feelings to him, he joyfully in-
vokes Heaven for having pulled him from the ranks of the wretched
and for shaping an enviable future for him. And though he concludes
that the realm of the senses appealed to him more than his abstract
theories, he learns that love alone cannot insure his happiness, for he
becomes aware that when two persons see each other continually, the
result of familiarity causes the ardor of love to diminish. As a married
man, Cleveland is accepted by society and has an adoring wife. He
has few external obstacles to overcome but nonetheless recognizes that
he lacks something for complete inner peace. Separated from Fanny,
he dreams of being near her but finds her constant attentiveness stifling and longs for solitude. To resolve the dilemma of passion, which
he believes both necessary to his happiness and impossible to control,
Cleveland attempts at times to deny all feeling.

The Primacy of Feeling

The other principal characters are affected by extremes of feelings
in equally absolute terms. Fanny conceives of happiness entirely in
terms of love, which is for her the supreme good. Cleveland views
love at times as a malediction, the source of all his suffering, the
most terrible of all his evils. Since he believes, however, that love is
necessary to his happiness, he rails against Providence and denies responsibility for the course of his destiny in view of the seemingly total disproportion between virtue and reward. The example of Gelin,
Cleveland's friend who betrays and vilifies both Cleveland and Fanny,
is representative of a seemingly capricious and cruel universe in which
the good suffer the most. Since Fanny "needed only love and virtue

to be happy" (571), the anguish she experiences at being victimized by Gelin's treachery when he suggests that Cleveland is in love with Mme Lallin literally consumes her. Having staked all her hopes for happiness on love, she rushes to the cloisters when her expectations fail to materialize, hoping to find a peace in the contemplation of the divinity that her worldly experiences have not provided. After the death of her daughter, she embraces the Catholic faith, ostensibly because its strict hierarchy of dogmas and tenets addresses matters concerning man and God and entrusts to the domain of Providence what is clearly beyond human understanding. Fanny's inability to fathom the ways of the universe is underscored by her final indictment of the human condition, and it is her bitterness that pervades the final tableau of a prolonged itinerary, she who had defined herself in terms of her need to love.

Gelin, who appears to embody Elizabeth Cleveland's warnings against the dangers of uncontrolled passion, lies, cheats, and betrays Cleveland's trust and almost achieves his goal of poisoning Cleveland's marriage by his malicious lies. In his apparent regeneration and the tone of repentance that marks his self-accusation, he nevertheless suggests that he should not be held responsible for the "fatal passion that devours me." He shudders with shame at the thought of the depths to which he had fallen and reveals that, like Cleveland, he views the excesses of passion as part of the natural order gone awry (371). Gelin states that he was always convinced that "nature had infallible resources to give birth to and inflame the passions" whereas Cleveland tells his adversary that he understands how violent passion can make a man stray from his duty (465). Yet Cleveland's vaunted philosophical stoicism had clearly broken down, as indicated by his violent transports when he believes he has incontrovertible proof of Fanny's infidelity. Linking love with misfortune and cursing his life, he contemplates suicide. Monty points out that Cleveland, as his journey progresses, is forced to distinguish between the theory and practice of love and reason.[8] When he is separated from Fanny whom he believes unfaithful and he falls in love with Cécile who, unknown to him is his daughter, he does not hesitate to make the break between marriage and love: "Our desires were the same: the cry of honor and virtue was not strong enough to make itself heard" (328). Abandoning a sheltered cave may indeed make the individual the victim of human inconstancy and excessive passions but it is this feeling that affirms existence itself. Nowhere is the link between feeling and life expressed more clearly than at the moment when Cleveland, in the presence of Cécile, receives a note from the "unfaithful" Fanny. Gasping for breath, he notes: ". . . my troubled imagination no longer represented anything to me but confusedly. I had neither ideas nor distinct feelings. I remained for a few moments in this state . . ." (343).

Earlier he had experienced the opportunity of viewing his past misfortunes parade before his eyes. Believing Mme Riding and his daughter dead and Fanny adulterous, he had refused to accede to total pessimism. Despite all evidence to the contrary, Cleveland remains convinced that his faith in the salutary power of love, the society of men, and human reason will be justified. Plunged into the darkest melancholy when he learns of Gelin's deceptions and the consequences of Gelin's treachery, Cleveland no longer feels able to rely on reason to elucidate the mysteries surrounding him.

Reunited with Fanny who, through Gelin's confession, has been absolved of all attacks and having been avenged by his enemies, Cleveland has gained much self-knowledge through his sufferings. Although he has long rejected philosophy as a viable system that would allow him to remain unscathed in a world beset by social evils, natural disasters, and inexplicable twists of fortune, he turns to religion as a means of securing the inner peace that, opposing theoretical formulas, can emanate only from the self. He has attained Fanny's love and is prepared to live with her in relative tranquillity but he has buried a daughter and endured too much pain to rely on theories. If his odyssey reveals that passion is more powerful than philosophy, it suggests no less forcefully that love and affection can never guarantee happiness and that happiness, itself reflecting the complexities of man's drives and needs, is consequently subject to infinite qualifications.

The image Cleveland evokes in describing his life to Mylord Clarendon is a microcosm of the Prévostean world, one in which the individual, falling in the deepest part of a river, attempts unsuccessfully to station himself against the onrushing waters (508). Significantly, the voyager, driven by the force of nature, loses control but does not drown. Equally significant is the fact that the closing words of the novel are spoken not by Cleveland but by Fanny who, weeping openly over her daughter's grave, reveals her thoughts on the misery of the human condition. Cleveland, like Beckett's Krapp, remains silent in the background, his earlier philosophic temerity having been replaced by the only possible certainty, one that looks ahead to Candide and his garden, that man must liberate himself from metaphysical worry about the problem of evil by means of action.

The Limits of Philosophy

Although *Cleveland* is Prévost's most philosophical novel in the sense that its hero is obsessed with formulating a theory of life encompassing nature, feeling, reason, society, and religion, it reveals that Prévost was an unsystematic philosopher who distrusted abstractions which were removed from everyday practical experience. Like the Voltaire of the *Traité de métaphysique* of 1734, Prévost believed that God is an omnipotent being and that the liberty of His creatures is related to His own liberty. At the same time Prévost upheld that extraordinarily sensitive individuals are often overtaken by passions they are unable to control. A note of ambiguity surrounds Prévost's ideas on free will. Man is free but he can never entirely master all his desires. Men are governed by a general Providence by the very nature of their finitude, but are responsible for particular social evils that threaten their well-being.

Prévost unequivocally viewed man as a social animal and, like Rousseau, was preoccupied with describing the conditions whereby the private person could function with tranquillity within the larger social framework. Prévost depicts characters repeatedly overpowered both by the strength of their passion and the unexpected changes in their lives engendered by the actions of others. Mary Ford has described "le bonheur du repos" (the happiness of repose) as "the tranquil contentment of the solitary human being," associated with cloisters, caverns, gardens, fields, and woods.[9] There are few choices in Prévost between this movement of retreat and the kind of involvement in society that makes the individual more vulnerable to the passions. When Cleveland expresses his fears at abandoning the solitary life of Rumney-Hole, Axminster tells him that he will have to accommodate his virtues to the ways of the world. Despite his initial fears about entering society, however, Cleveland soon comes to place a high value on friendship. His own principles of generosity and justice, we learn, were both kindled by the alleged charitable acts of others, and he is capable of being moved to tears by his father-in-law's acts of kindness and generosity. Toward the end of his spiritual voyage he views the friendship of Mylord Clarendon as necessary to his finding peace and later reflects, while at a banquet table, how much pleasure he derives from the thought that he is in part responsible for the happiness of others. Yet Cleveland recognizes that no single component of his life, be it love, friendship, study, or solitude, can ever satisfy him entirely because the human personality is constantly evolving.

Elizabeth Cleveland takes pains to teach her son that he should not hate life but rather the miseries to which it exposes man, adding that there would be little to pity in man's condition if he would only avail himself of what is useful to his happiness. Before leaving his cave, Cleveland had conceived of happiness as a fixed, inalterable state. Convinced both of the efficacy of the powers of reason and of his unique sensibility, he believes that it is possible to reconcile virtue with the object of his passion through the intervention of reason. As a result of his experiences it will become increasingly evident, as Claude Roquin has noted, that the philosophe and the sensitive man do not coincide.[10]

At the outset of his apprenticeship in life Cleveland believes that men are capable of controlling their destiny and achieving happiness. At the beginning of Book 3 he has endured a violent storm and shipwreck in crossing from England to France, discovers a plot against Mylord Axminster by Mme Lallin's brother, but is knighted by Charles II and sees preparations for his marriage to Fanny. He recognizes, however, that philosophy has been of little value in appeasing his inner pains because "a philosopher is a man first and foremost by his emotions" (85). Recognition of this truth does not provide the inner peace he so desperately seeks, and because he is thoroughly convinced that men have a right to be happy, he is loath to accept the conclusions of his experiences. This Hamlet-in-reverse has decided that the cause of what is rotten in the world must lie not in the world but in himself. Whereas the optimism of Voltaire's Pangloss results in a state of moral intransigeance, a passive acceptance of evil in the name of a cosmic order that transcends man's understanding, Cleveland reacts to the ways of man in precisely the opposite fashion, believing that he has within himself the capacity to create order in both the world and in himself. In his desire to explain all, to find reasons for everything he encounters, Cleveland frequently intensifies the absurd. Hearing from Mme Riding of the Rouintons' cruelty, he reflects: "I am looking for reasons to justify their barbarous acts" (229). After he and his company have been taken prisoner by the Rouintons and his half-brother Bridge has been killed by Gelin in a duel, Cleveland makes a final effort to ward off total despair as he settles in the city of Saumur: ". . . I had something more consoling to expect from my reason. Although the resources that it offered me were still powerless, I knew at least by the experience of the past that if my present evils were not absolutely incurable, it was from it [reason] alone that I was supposed to hope for the cure" (278). By this point, however, Cleveland's reliance on reason is a rhetorical exercise and it is only the strongest act of will that prevents him from committing suicide. When he concludes that reason is of no use in elucidating the mysteries surrounding him, he ascribes ultimate control of human destiny to Providence and thus hints at what will be his final posture as he gradually emerges from his extreme melancholy: the contemplation of the divine to divert his attention from the total chaos of human society. The mind, Cleveland concludes, loses its force in subjugating itself to the senses. Elizabeth Cleveland's vaunted equilibrium has proved to be chimerical, and Cleveland, exhausted, confused, and unhappy, turns to God when forced to admit the utter incomprehensibility of the temporal order.

The Utopias

Cleveland's inability to find the inner peace promised by his mother's teachings directly influences the rhythm of the novel, for Cleveland comes to pursue his goal with increasingly greater fervor. Happiness at Rumney-Hole was envisaged in terms of maintaining absolute control of the environment. Elizabeth Cleveland was able to live in peace at the price of withdrawing from society. In their travels Cleveland, Bridge (Cleveland's half-brother whose mother had also been Cromwell's mistress), and Mme Riding have the opportunity to observe firsthand societies that have been able to maintain their political-economic-social standards only by willfully cutting themselves off from the rest of society. The ultimate disillusionment that Cleveland and his friends experience in the Rochellois community and among the Abaquis and Nopandes underscores a central motif of the novel, the clash between the real and the ideal, between individual and collective happiness.

The dictionary definition of *utopia* points to the inherent contradictions of the term: 1) an ideally perfect place especially in its sociopolitical standards; 2) an impractical, idealistic concept for social and political reform.[11] Because they are ideals, utopias can be upheld as models for men to emulate, but it is axiomatic that the very qualities that make utopias ideal make them unfit for human society. Sean Harrington states that utopia represented for Prévost the ideal of universal happiness and social harmony to be achieved within the human community.[12] Prévost's harsh criticism of Thomas More's *Utopia* in the *Pour et contre* leaves little doubt that he believed in the amelioration of human society at large and disdained the narrow view of utopia as represented by the simple cell-like structure of Rumney-Hole—what Harrington views as a solution "that equates happiness with peace and quiet among a select, isolated few . . ."[13] In her teachings Elizabeth Cleveland had pitted nature and reason against society and the passions. Wisdom and virtue, according to her scheme, were both influenced by reason, and the wise philosopher would be prepared to wage a constant battle to temper the passions. Cleveland concludes that men voluntarily bring misery upon themselves, for nature intended them to be happy but their passions destroy their peace of mind.

The whole question of utopias was very much in vogue in eighteenth-century literature, for the problem had universal ramifications involving theories of progress, the relative merits of primitive man and civilized man, nature as opposed to art, and individual happiness in the context of the common weal. Virtually all the major Enlightenment writers were interested in the subject and wrote about it extensively.

The Rochellois colony. Philip Stewart writes that the first utopia, the Rochellois colony near St. Helena where Bridge and five companions go, fulfills Louis Marin's definition that a utopia always situates itself in the midst of a historical contradiction.[14] The Rochellois colony, moreover, like every utopia, according to Marin's definition, combines antagonistic tendencies without synthesizing or resolving them and therefore bears within itself the nondialectic potential for self-destruction.

The Rochellois community, founded by French Huguenots in search of religious freedom, resembles in its physical characteristics Voltaire's Eldorado. Both are secluded from the rest of the world and the Rochellois colony maintains, as Harrington observes, a "pristine, utopian purity free of contamination from the outside world, principally the colonial powers of Europe that were a source of decadence and corruption.[15] Bridge and his friends find themselves on the island because of Mme Eliot, who had been sent to find men to populate the colony.

Bridge's first impression of this island society is positive. An inhabitant tells him that they live in the community without fear, like children in their father's house. Four governors, he learns, are elected every year to maintain the public weal. When they arrived from Europe the Huguenots were rich in silver, but soon learned tht money was of little value there in view of the need for practical necessities. The Rochellois boast of their perfect equality because they adhere to the concept of common property. In placing greater value on the essence of politeness rather than on its outer manifestation, the Rochellois seem to have progressed beyond superficial European customs. It is apparent, however, that this society is seriously flawed in several respects. The three parts of the family unit—fathers, children, and servants—are based on an unequal division of labor characterized by servants and masters. The community is governed by a council of elders, a gerontocracy whose prime interest is that of preserving and guaranteeing the transfer of power from one elite group to the next, a state of affairs that Stewart calls "a caste system with benevolent paternalism."[16] Even the isolation of the island has negative implications inasmuch as it suggests, like the Rumney-Hole cell, an inability to function within the greater human society, but, more significantly, like Eldorado, it has the effect of creating an atmosphere of a prison from which escape is neither sanctioned nor easily accomplished.

The Rochellois community is flawed most seriously by its failure to accommodate individual needs to the dictates of the society-at-large. Because the community believes it has to be on constant guard against destructive human passions, it stifles all individual freedom. Bridge and his five companions rebel against their having to marry women chosen by lot, thus upholding their right to follow the dictates of their hearts. It seems likely that Prévost wished to emphasize the fundamentally unresolved tensions that exist between the individual and the community in all utopias. Sgard, commenting on the Rochellois incident, concludes that the happiness of the island is not based on virtue, that love and the social order remain irreconcilable and that this is no Happy Island because in Prévost's mind there is no happiness without love.[17]

That the island indeed contains within it the seeds of its own destruction is evidenced in the epidemic in which the population is decimated and the vaunted ideal of isolation and self-sufficiency is rendered totally useless. Like all utopias, the Rochellois community offers no challenge for mankind inasmuch as its inhabitants have settled down for the perpetuation of a way of life that they do not choose to alter. Conformity rather than growth is the dominant characteristic of the island. Bridge's inability to limit his field of action reveals a deep-seated human need. The Rochellois community is therefore not an ideal that men can imitate because it constricts man's innate drives. The inhabitants have paid the price of being dehumanized for their lack of external conflict. By their departure Bridge and his group show that freedom and its corollaries—movement and change— are basic to human life. In the world of the Rochellois community the concept of benevolence itself has been abstracted inasmuch as it results from a negation of all emotional affect. Motivation with respect to growth and change is nonexistent in a society whose inhabitants have settled down for the perpetuation of the status quo. The self-destructive element of the community lies in its insistence on adhering to a changeless order, which implies a rejection of man's finitude. The quick demise of the community, moreover, as a result of the epidemic, suggests that the survival of the species, both in quantitative and qualitative terms, lies in the interdependence of all nations.

The Abaquis.   Cleveland's stay among the Abaquis ostensibly provides an opportunity for Prévost to examine the relative merits of two cultures, a primitive society and European civilization, or what Stewart calls "the imposition of one culture on another."[18] Although Cleveland ingratiates himself sufficiently with the Abaquis to be chosen their lawgiver and commander-in-chief, thus performing what James Gilroy sees as a double role of mentor and Télémaque, it is clear that enlightened benevolence is not his sole motivation in remaining among these Indians and that his primary interest is to build a powerful army that will allow him to come to his father-in-law's aid.[19]

Cleveland's reflections on the course of human destiny and on his own life in particular prior to this episode suggest that he is still vacillating between extremes in his quest for happiness. The same Cleveland who comments on the great range of feeling that an individual is capable of experiencing because of the contingencies of life announces shortly thereafter that the study of wisdom will be his only occupation. Before the Abaquis episode Cleveland had repeatedly la-

mented human instability as evidenced in a dichotomy between what
men profess to be and what they are in reality, between abstract theories about balancing passion, reason, and virtue and the proof of
misery all about him. During his stay among the Abaquis Cleveland
himself demonstrates that all concepts of virtue and vice must constantly be reassessed in terms of human relativity. The Abaquis episode is therefore of major importance because it foreshadows
Cleveland's final stance before the problem of human happiness.

Cleveland's condescending attitude toward the Abaquis surfaces in
several instances. Although he expresses his shock at the Abaquis's
nudity, he admits that the shame he feels at being naked wasn't a
natural feeling. These same people appear stupid to him because he
believes that they are indifferent to their own self-preservation. He
theorizes, moreover, that they are flattering him because they believe
he is superior to them. His arrival dramatizes changes in the Abaquis's way of life. Sun worshippers, they disdained all formal ritual
and did not even feel compelled to assemble for religious purposes.
The deism that Cleveland sought to impose in place of sun worship-
ping was guided by principles of wisdom and reason—belief in and
submission to a Supreme Being, punishment for sins, and the reci-
tation of brief prayers in a general assembly twice weekly and daily
in the home—but Cleveland's personal interests, his love for Fanny,
and his concern for her father's welfare, take precedence over his desire to put into practice the principles he had learned from books,
blending natural philosophy and moral religion. Confessing to feeling
flattered by the Abaquis's attention, he recognizes the need to extract
obedience from them and devises a system of rigid punishment which
would be meted out to those who violate his trust.

Cleveland discovers that the Abaquis's natural proclivity to a tranquil existence within their own tribe—"quarrels and divisions were
almost unknown among them"—was sullied by their ongoing wars
with the fierce Rouintons. Cleveland's contact with the Abaquis
teaches him that events in human history frequently cannot withstand
rational scrutiny inasmuch as there is little connection between intent
and result and, more specifically, between virtue and happiness. His
real education involves among other things a growing awareness that
man in society must lead a life in which his own destiny is much
influenced by the passions of others.

As ruler, Cleveland undertakes a number of steps that drastically change the Abaquis's manner of life. Lacking honor and wealth, the Abaquis had neither hope nor desire. They therefore react with both fear and awe to the rank that they themselves impose on him. He realizes, nonetheless, that it will be difficult to rule these people because they have never had to yield to authority and it would be necessary to extract obedience from them. Cleveland's desire to be lawgiver and chief is not entirely dictated by personal interest, for he takes pains to tell Youngster that he has no claim to power and even less to tyranny. Gilroy compares Cleveland here to Fénelon's protagonist in trying to create an orderly, pious, and peaceful community, taking reason and nature as his guides.[20]

Noting that filial respect was in no way obligatory, Cleveland attempted to impose a system of paternal authority, formed a council of elders, and divided the nation into twenty parts, establishing authority over the economic life as well as the social order by supervising the distribution of all economic goods. The inherent contradictions of Cleveland's system touched all facets of the Abaquis's life. Having known freedom and equality without having felt the constraint of any formal authority, the Abaquis are suddenly confronted by a lawgiver who capitalizes on their fear of the Rouintons in order to keep the young Abaquis in check. Admitting his ignorance of the study of arms, Cleveland attempts to lead the Abaquis to battle against their enemy while condemning war as a blot on reason and humanity. Harrington assesses the failure of Cleveland's ideology in terms of a fundamental clash between the real and the ideal.[21] The breakdown of Cleveland's principles of moderation becomes clear when his personal rancor at Moou's rebellion leads him to use Moou's death as proof of his invincible power against those who defy his authority, and he points to Moou as a hint of future malediction. The Abaquis, in fact, willingly abandon their sun worship after Moou's death and adopt a system of belief in an omnipotent, invisible God who, in Cleveland's words, "moves the heavens and makes the earth tremble" (211). The futility of Cleveland's efforts to mold an entire people according to his own vision is heightened symbolically by the Rouintons's choosing to destroy their land rather than fall under Cleveland's domination and by the mysterious illness that kills half of Cleveland's troops.

For all his good intentions Cleveland brings his own kind of moral decay to the Abaquis, the sin of presumption. For Stewart the balance sheet is entirely negative: the Indians lose everything they had known before Cleveland's arrival—no obedience to authority, no organized religion, peace, equality, freedom. Because of this, Stewart feels that it was more of a utopia before Cleveland arrived.[22]

The Abaquis episode examines several key questions in the novel. What emerges here is not so much whether man is capable of attaining happiness but rather whether he is capable of recognizing where his greatest potential for happiness lies. It is not, moreover, a question of the white man's failure to elevate the noble savage, for, as Mary Ford points out, the Abaquis were virtuous and reasonable by European standards.[23] Sociability may be a basic human instinct but it can also provide the conditions whereby man's basest desires fester. Cleveland, essentially a virtuous man, attempts to expose "natural feelings" to these people, including filial respect and a horror of infanticide. The Abaquis episode does not end on a totally pessimistic note but only, as Robert Mauzi states, because of Prévost's avoiding all monochromatic hues in depicting either Cleveland or the Indians.[24]

The Abaquis episode provides a moment in time when the attainment of significant political and social reform seems possible. Yet the Abaquis, whom Cleveland regards merely as instruments of his will, obey their new leader only because they fear the wrath of God. Cleveland, in turn, is forced to remain among these people. It is only through instances of physical and moral evil, an epidemic and a war, that the end of the episode reaches fruition.

The Nopandes. The third utopia, the kingdom of the Nopandes, witnessed by Mme Riding, reflects a strong Spanish influence, even to religious practices, we are told. Although Mme Riding was ignorant of the origins of their religion, she intuitively felt that the Nopandes's establishments were based more on practical considerations than on superstition. A rigid system of punishment was meted out to those who had wounded the divine majesty, the authority of the prince, and public safety.

The price paid for this state of royal absolutism, in which order appears to reign supreme, is an exclusivity, a remoteness that resembles the Eldorado of Voltaire's *Candide*. The system of punishment established among these nations evokes for Stewart a "decadent Christianity retaining only its fetish-like saints and statues and no notion whatever of spirituality.'"[25] Because it was their contact with the Spaniards that fifty years ago changed this nation from an anarchical barbaric people into one with a tightly organized system of laws, the

Nopandes seem openly receptive to the principle of change and react favorably to Mme Riding's suggestions on how they can be more just in the application of their laws. The kind of royal absolutism and Christianity practiced by the Nopandes dramatizes the problem of reconciling two potentially antithetical conditions—the conformity that results from a highly structured society based on a system of absolute power from above and the rights of the individual to maintain his distinct qualities.

Despite Mme Riding's glowing praise for the Nopandes kingdom, which she describes as "the greatest perhaps and the most polite which exists in the universe," there is evidence to support the claim that the outward serenity of a nation living in physical and psychological isolation masks volatile passions that lie dormant and ultimately surface. Moou's passion for Fanny led him to rebel against all external constraints. When the prince of the Nopandes falls in love with Cécile he refuses to assist Mme Riding in her departure. Love and order remain unreconciled and Mme Riding continues her search for family and friends.

Mauzi writes that Prévost distinguishes between "ideal nature," the highest expression of civilized man, and "historical nature," that one associates with the condition of primitives.[26] Civilization reflects the totality of nature which, as Sgard points out, is "a chaos of good and bad instincts."[27] The community of the Nopandes practices concepts of morality and reason. Yet it is clearly no model for humanity inasmuch as its self-imposed physical and psychological isolation implies that whatever enlightenment it has achieved can be maintained only at the price of protecting its inhabitants from themselves and from the rest of the world. The peace and harmony Mme Riding describes so glowingly exists within a community whose remoteness evokes the cave of Rumney-Hole and that, like this earlier setting, clashes with man's need for freedom. The Nopandes episode tells us also that the conflict between claims of the individual will dominate those of any theoretical ideology.

The esteem and gratitude Mme Riding felt for the Nopandes made her wish to say with these people, but she ultimately decided that she could not ignore the opportunity to relieve her suffering and she therefore left the community. It is true that the prince embraces Mme Riding's advice on achieving great happiness but wishes to limit this state of greater enlightenment to specified boundaries. Mme Riding rebels and reenters a world where contingency and irrationality abound, perhaps not the best of all possible worlds but the only one possible.

The Rochellois community ignored man's passions, the Abaquis refused Cleveland's reforms, and the Nopandes achieve law and order through negative means—the threat of punishment—rather than through natural wisdom. Man and his societies are capable of amelioration but earthly paradises are completely foreign to the human condition.

Conclusion

Until the final conversion under Mylord Clarendon's influence, Cleveland had always approached religion in an entirely unsystematic way. Because of his mother's experiences and preachings he could not ignore the possibility that very real dangers lay ahead for him as he left the tomb-like existence of Rumney-hole. Equally convinced, however, that man's purpose in life is to be happy and that man has the capacity to shape his destiny, he suggests by his invoking of Providence that the incidents of bad fortune in his life can be attributed to a force beyond his comprehension, a power that orders the universe in a general way. He views Paradise, not in terms of orthodox theology—the doctrine of eternal life—but entirely in earthly terms, an "eternity of happiness and love." As long as Cleveland believes that he can be happy in the society of men he feels little need to turn to metaphysics as an aid in his life's goal. His thoughts during a storm at sea just after he leaves his mother's cave are typical of his stance. Believing that the mysteries of the world can be elucidated by the powers of reason, he implores Providence not to expose him to evils that he will not be able to understand. As we have shown, Cleveland's spiritual odyssey is a record of growing disenchantment with his mother's philosophy and an acceptance of the limits of reason. Experiences of love and society had led Cleveland to conclusions far removed from those of his mother. The religion he preached as leader of the Abaquis had already evolved from a rationally based deism positing the existence of God as the clock-maker creator of the universe and formed instead the basis for a religion of nature, much more aligned to the heart than to the mind. God, the Supreme Being, must be honored as the sole master of love and His creatures must be loved because they are His work.

It is apparent, however, that Cleveland's religion of the heart is insufficient to provide comfort in the wake of catastrophic events. Reunited with Fanny and exhausted both mentally and physically from his paroxysms of anger, jealousy, and fear, he addresses all his griefs to Providence. He later reflects on the harsh capriciousness of Providence for causing him to endure such rigorous tests before knowing its benefits. The marvels of the same Providence are extolled when Cleveland learns that Cécile had gone to France with Mme Riding and was therefore not lost.

Providence here is synonymous with fate or destiny, the result of the complex, ever-changing interaction between his own life and the lives of others in his immediate circle and without. Cleveland's religion, which influences his final evolution under Clarendon's aegis, is properly speaking neither doctrinaire Catholicism nor Protestantism, for Cleveland recognizes that religious establishments have not caused him to know goodness and justice and he therefore avoids metaphysical theories that are aligned exclusively with one particular sect. Prévost's disinclination to accede to a thoroughgoing pessimism is implied in Cleveland's shifting attitudes toward religion. Like Pierre Bayle, Prévost the defrocked priest walked along a path of skepticism, unprepared to state that man could be held responsible for sin if God is all-perfect. Ultimately he submitted that human reason is incapable of understanding the relationship between God and man, that the human mind cannot fathom the problem of evil. When Mylord Clarendon confronts a weary Cleveland and alludes to the limits of reason in certain matters, he finds an attentive listener. Clarendon holds before Cleveland not the certainty of eternal life for the faithful but permanent principles of justice and morality that are impervious to worldly vicissitudes. Cleveland's announced hierarchy of values at the conclusion of the novel reveals the centrality of religion, the contemplation beyond the self, in his view of man's condition. The inclinations of the heart occupy the first rank, but religious and social duties, including the cultivation of friendship, are also emphasized.

The Final Stance.   The conclusion of the novel points in two directions. On the one hand, Cleveland does not turn to religion as a source of potential happiness because he knows that he will forever remain ignorant of the reasons for man's having been put on earth. Yet, as Carroll notes, Cleveland turns to religion to provide him with a certainty that philosophy cannot justify.[28] He is able to provide Clarendon with undeniable proofs of rampant evil and irrational occurrences in the world and dwells so long on the negative incidents in his life precisely because of their inexplicable and unforeseen nature. The final tableau, in which Fanny's anguished cry over the misery of the human condition is balanced by Cleveland's resolve not to give in to total despair, is, in R. A. Francis's view, not unlike Candide's cultivation of his garden, one that involves action and reintegration into the surrounding society.[29] Evil will of course continue to pervade Cleveland's world but, to the extent that it will not lead him to question the very meaning of existence, it will no longer be a problem for him. From the perspective of achieving understanding of the universe Cleveland is filled with a sense of the absurd, but the implications of his acceptance of what he cannot understand are far-reaching. The question of free will having been relegated to the domain of the pragmatic, to human action, the novel concludes on a somber note: For those who roam the world in search of ultimate meaning and inner tranquillity, the greatest possibility of exhilarating discovery lies in the recognition and acceptance of human finitude.

Because the possibilities of human understanding and action are limited, all fixed and absolute theories and judgments are antithetical to man's nature. Gelin repents sufficiently to curse the excesses of passion that led him to betray a trusted friend. Gelin's "conversion" does not efface his past behavior but it does suggest that if men are endowed with reason this innate reason must be nurtured by civilization. Because of the non-innate quality of evil, there is always the possibility that men who have been corrupt can be influenced by examples of virtue and reason in other men. Prévost affirms the principle of sociability in *Cleveland* by showing not that society corrupts men but rather than men corrupt society.

Cleveland is an open-ended novel in the sense that nothing has been "solved." Cleveland, the English philosophe, has been forced to abandon all absolute theories about man's place in the universe. The depiction of human limitations with respect to reason comes about only because Cleveland, like his predecessor des Grieux, dreams of an existence in which passion, virtue, and society meet in perfect harmony. Cleveland's reliance on divine Providence implies not only the recognition of these limitations but also an awareness of the gulf between the ideal and the real. His stance near the tomb of his daughter and his rejection of all abstractions evoke, however, not only a sense of the absurd but, most significantly, the grandeur of man with respect to the scope of his aspirations and the price he pays when, at the end of his long voyage, he comes to accept limited victories. It is the specter of the tomb, a mood of resignation and quiet despair, that surfaces in the conclusion, an unambiguous assertion that solitary and social man, reasoning and feeling man, will forever be ignorant of the ultimate meaning of human existence.

Chapter Six
A Worldly Cleric:
Le Doyen de Killerine

Le Doyen and Prévost's Other Works

The *Avant-Propos.* *Le Doyen de Killerine: Histoire morale* (The dean of Killerine: A moral history), Prévost's last long novel, appears to follow in the tradition of the earlier works. Like Renoncour, the dean is "established" in the world, but is forced to examine his principles in the light of his new role as mentor and moral guide to his half-siblings following their father's death. As in earlier works, Prévost focuses on the question of the individual's happiness, and his protagonist-narrator preaches the wisdom of adhering to a code of behavior that he feels is harmonious with the laws of the Church and with the honor, virtue, and ultimate happiness of his family. One might well be tempted to conclude that Prévost intended this work to stand as a companion piece to *Cleveland.*

The *Avant-Propos* ("Foreword") to *Le Doyen* contains the obligatory defense of the author's moral intentions, this time specifically with respect to *Cleveland* in which Prévost insists he was unjustly accused of having undermined morality. Some critics, on the other hand, have cautioned against interpreting the end of *Cleveland* as proof of the triumph of religion, for, as Carroll points out, Clarendon's claims for religion offer Cleveland no more certainty than philosophy had, and in fact Clarendon is able to exert an influence on Cleveland only because the study of philosophy has yielded neither absolute truths nor happiness.[1] Despite Suzanne Carroll's reservations, others, perhaps influenced by the fact that the title *Le Doyen de Killerine* evokes a religious office and that the subtitle, *Histoire morale,* alludes to a dialectic between codes of behavior linked to Church and state and the claims of passion, have interpreted Prévost's self-defense more literally. Monty sees in *Le Doyen* the attempt to amplify the principles of *Cleveland,* "to reconcile the conflict between the Christian and the

honnête homme, between religion and the world."[2] Henri Coulet, noting that the dean has not yet been tested in the real world, stresses
nonetheless that this character possesses from the very beginning the
truths that Cleveland attained only at the end of his arduous journey,
thus implying not only that the doyen enjoys a spiritual kinship with
the protagonist of the earlier novel but also that he is singularly well
prepared to act as an arbiter in matters of morality.[3]

Literary influences.   In her insightful study of Prévost Carol
Marie Lazzaro has discussed at length what she sees as one of the main
stumbling blocks in approaches to *Le Doyen de Killerine* (and *Cleveland*), "the lack of a proper literary perspective through which to
view Prévost."[4] Lazzaro concludes that Prévost should be placed in
the tradition of the romance as practiced both by the ancient Greeks
and their French imitators in the sixteenth and seventeenth centuries.
Lazzaro explains that in the Romance tradition man is constantly involved in a power struggle either against society or some more powerful figure than he and he is therefore forced to try to escape with
what he can get on earth or be satisfied with what is dictated to him.[5]
The very basis of the romance, then, in Lazzaro's view militates
against the emergence of a philosophical hero. Pointing out that the
romance has always had a greater affinity with comedy than with
tragedy, Lazzaro takes exception to those who, like Sgard, see in *Le
Doyen* the resurgence of Prévost's basic pessimism.

Far from being an example of a failed experiment, the novel reveals
a Voltairean spirit in its depiction of complex human desires and the
resulting spirit of the absurd. This is a universe where the incommensurate is the rule, where there are always unresolved disparities
between both intent and action and action and result, and where virtuous behavior itself is never a guarantee of happiness. The Pantagruelism that emerges in this work as an invitation to accept
imperfect human nature never degenerates into moral intransigeance,
an acceptance of human depravity in the name of an unknown greater
good, as embodied in Pangloss's attitude. Like Voltaire, Prévost in
Le Doyen de Killerine is an anti-Pangloss, who condemns not the imperfections by which man is defined but rather the mediocrity of
never aspiring to greater heights.

The world of relative values.   During the eighteenth century
in France there was a growing breach between the traditional ideal of
virtue and vice and man's social behavior. In the medieval world view
virtue was defined in terms of a retreat from society, an inward call

to contemplation of the divine, which stood in firm opposition to worldly pursuits. Since the eighteenth century rejected the idea of original sin and replaced it with the idea of man's perfectibility, it believed that virtue had to be social in nature. Whereas the Jesuit-Jansenist controversies in *Cleveland* allowed Prévost to demonstrate that casuistry and intellectual deception are not limited to any one sect, theological discussions in *Le Doyen* take a secondary position to the main interest which is psychological. As a political exile throughout most of the narrative, the dean attempts to formulate codes of worldly behavior for his family to emulate that do not conflict with the tenets of religion. Although the fictitious editor of the novel saw the work revolving around an opposition between religion and honor, Lazzaro has pointed out that critics have felt the need to explain why Prévost does not succeed in showing through the dean how religion can and must guide the average man in his dealings with the world.[6] Lazzaro goes on to state what is at the crux of the matter, namely, that the dean never articulates any specific moral or religious principles. Indeed, the dean is a mentor without a planned program, a family leader whose background and oath of celibacy make him singularly ill equipped to deal with passion. Although he speaks frequently of honor and virtue, the very vagueness of his principles gives these words a hollow ring. As family head of his half-siblings, he will increasingly reveal, nevertheless, that utopic retreats from society are inconsonant with human nature and that the wise individual is he who is able to bend his general principles to fit specific circumstances.

   Portrait of the dean.   The description of the dean at the beginning of the novel as a man with hooked legs, a hunched back, a face disfigured by two warts, and a very large head, establishes the theme of the absurd. Here is a man who has been dealt a cruel blow by nature. William Mead has theorized that Prévost as a lover emerged in *Manon Lescaut* whereas Prévost the moralist is exemplified by the dean. Mead goes on to say that Prévost's intent was not to satirize morality by associating it with a man who had the look of a "Moses in poodle-peruke and clerical gown" or by implication to give it serious credence, but rather to show the dynamic influence of two kinds of wisdom on each other—the dean's unworldly, as opposed to Georges's worldly, wisdom.[7]

   The dean is at first a naive cleric whose simplistic approach to worldly matters is suggested by the terms he uses to designate his siblings: Georges is quick and decisive, Patrice recognizes others' talents, and Rose is sweet. Since the dean's stated mission, finding suitable spouses for each of the three siblings, involves contact with society, he will, in a typical situation for Prévost's narrators, be as much educated in the ways of the world as exercising the role of mentor. Lazzaro has pointed out the discrepancy between the dean's actions and the religious and moral principles he thinks he is following.[8] At no time, however, is the dean able to entertain the thought of a prolonged retreat from the world, and his brief flight into Ireland comes to an end the moment he fears for his family's well-being. Far from being a deformed buffoon who hides behind abstract theories, he becomes increasingly a crafty man of the world who surreptitiously is able to manipulate others to accomplish what he believes is a greater good. Unlike Cleveland, the dean hardly agonizes over philosophical questions such as man's destiny, free will, and the meaning of existence. Nevertheless, he is far from being portrayed as a crass clergyman, reminiscent of the Jesuits of Prévost's earlier novels.

In the Preface Prévost stated what was for him the key problem facing the dean, determining the degree to which a Christian can give himself over to the world. Unlike Cleveland who leaves Rumney-Hole filled with distrust of society, the dean is confident in his family's ability to use reason in their pursuit of happiness within society. As a representative of formal religion, the dean appears to be markedly unconcerned about reconciling God's goodness and omnipotence with the reality of social evil. The dean is a spokesman of relativism and accepts the fact that men are rarely capable of exercising total altruism or even that such behavior is desirable. A representative of Catholicism, he approaches the problem of evil from a worldly perspective. Men are governed by a general Providence by the very nature of their finitude, but men are responsible for particular social evils that threaten their well-being.

The Dean and Society

The monastery and the world.   Despite his inability to arrive at definitive, inviolable laws concerning honor and virtue, the dean considers himself to be the final arbiter in all matters concerning family morality, reminding his siblings that he consented to take them to Paris only on condition that they undertake nothing without having informed him and received his advice. At the same time he stresses repeatedly that he is no different from any other man and that the ecclesiastical and secular states are merely "two different ways of accomplishing the same duties."[9] Because his own actions reflect the fact that change is the hallmark of the human condition, his pronouncements on behalf of absolute higher laws and standards are difficult to take seriously, as in the case of his admonishing Rose to think of her soul when she announces that she wishes to attend a ball.

It soon becomes apparent that the dean is far removed from the ascetic, cloistered world of the monastery. His initial unwillingness to leave his native Ireland does not betray a deep-seated hostility to the world but hints rather at his own confusion about what the relation between religion and the social world should be. What is clear is that the dean shows himself increasingly prepared to abide by the rules of society and that these rules are in a constant state of flux, according to particular circumstances. Sensing above all the practical advantages of Rose's marrying des Pesses, he expresses his dismay at her refusal. Society is shown to be shaped by the force of the passions. Love is the most dominant, but greed and ambition are also very important. The dean learns in his worldly adventures that both the orientation and the intensity of the passions are not fixed and that those who show the greatest degree of flexibility in adapting to new circumstances will reap the greatest benefits.

Thus, having formed an affection for Sara, the dean does everything in his power to promote her marriage to Patrice, but not for purely altruistic motives. The dean, "armed with Sara's generous gifts," which will allow him to intervene on Rose's behalf, insists on couching his wishes in idealistic terms, namely that Patrice's acceptance of Sara will enable him (Patrice) to become the father and protector of his family (88). There is at this moment a typical blurring between the dean's desire to make recommendations about his siblings' choice of spouses and his enunciation of higher moral principles. He is in fact a practical opportunist who sets about to secure a marriage whose chief interest for him is its financial benefits. The conflict between his self-image and the reality that surfaces from his behavior is clearly seen when, in his efforts to change Patrice's mind about marrying Sara, he tells him first that esteem is the most solid foundation of marriage but later states that religion is the most sacred element. The dean views the ensuing marriage as the culmination of his family's spiritual and worldly interests, a sign of both the glory of Providence and his brother's happiness as well as his family's improved social standing.

It is not surprising that the dean's need to present himself as a stern guardian of conventional Church-bound morality increases in direct proportion to his entanglements with lay society. One might conclude, in fact, that his invocation of traits, never clearly articulated, which he associates with his clerical state, gives him a sense of security that allows him to assuage his conscience when his manipulation of his siblings does not conform to his vows of Christian piety. Thus, the dean finds it necessary to justify a great deal of his behavior because his actions are motivated by worldly concerns. His reflections on his decision to intervene on Rose's behalf are initially influenced by what he perceives to be the general role of men in relation to women ("... the duty of men being always to comfort the weaknesses of women in taking upon ourselves the greater part of the burden"; 150). Only incidentally is he stricken by the possibility that there may be a conflict between his worldly pursuits, in this case coming to his sister's aid, and his ecclesiastical state. The Dean confronts here his fundamental dilemma, the fact that the demands of man's social existence challenge the wisdom of adhering to strict religious principles. For Harrington, the novel represents a "harmonious synthesis of natural morality and of social prestige with religious sensitivity and traditional orthodoxy."[10] Significantly, however, when referring to his activities on Rose's behalf, the dean confesses that his training makes him thoroughly unprepared to deal with the practical exigencies of life: "... I thought how indecent it is for a man of the Church to get involved voluntarily in adventures whose circumstances his profession does not allow him to uphold entirely or to follow through to their conclusion" (150). Although the Dean is always aware of a discrepancy between his metaphysical and social mission, he never uses the ambiguity of his position as an excuse to withdraw into passive contemplation. He therefore actively works to restore the honor of his family's name through socially and politically prestigious marriages but, at the same time, continues to believe that the two realms can be integrated. He tells Patrice that religion doesn't teach that it is easy to overcome the passions that it condemns, but that it offers at all times all the hope that can assure the victory (164).

The limits of reason; the force of passion. The dean is unable to draw on specific theological doctrines to serve as a moral guide because he recognizes the complexities of man's social existence. He relies on relative, pragmatic solutions to social situations because he comes to understand that society is governed more by passion than by reason and therefore is outside the influence of abstract, fixed rules. The dean, in a word, comes to accede to what he realizes cannot be changed. Revealing that he reproached Anglesey for having thought that Linch could be appeased he adds: "Linch loved my sister . . . Should love be punished?" (177). Shortly after, the dean shows himself capable of dealing with others, proposing neither violence nor dissimulation to Linch, all the while questioning Linch's motives. This deformed priest is a born survivor, one who maintains confidence in his own strengths. His belief that he has been directly responsible for Patrice's controlling his passion is characteristic of an ameliorative vision whereby the dean comes both to accept human nature and to recognize that society is a potentially civilizing force that can induce men to continue their march toward utopia.

At times, however, the dean is loath to accept the conclusions that his experiences force him to make—that man by his excesses is responsible for much of his own misery. Recognizing that there is a constant thread of the absurd in the universe since so much of human experience defies rational analysis, the dean longs for a higher authority to which he can turn, Providence. Having had to defend Patrice's character against Fincer's accusations, which he believes just, and having received a letter from Linch that he fears portends violence, he asks plaintively if it is a sign of weakness to reason on the impenetrable dispositions of Providence. For a brief moment the dean becomes the quintessential erring mite described by Pascal and sees himself as a creature at the mercy of forces whose capacity to harm his family he cannot control: "I saw myself reduced to implore the pity of Providence. Is not the misfortune of my pitiful family at its height?" (190). This appeal to metaphysical truth is of fleeting duration, for the dean soon reveals how worldly he has become. Mlle de L . . . we read, had a profound effect on him and, as he leaves her, he is obsessed by her image and feels both shame and a desire for vengeance.

Unable to extinguish his own feelings and passions, he still wishes to present to society the outward image of a man whose actions conform to the strict bounds of orthodox religion. When he thinks at one point of taking Mlle de L . . . to an apartment with Patrice and Rose, he hesitates because he feels that propriety would be transgressed. More often, however, as in the case when he contemplates encouraging Sara to marry Patrice a second time, he admits that he is now unsure of his own standards: "I am ignorant myself of what I condemn or what I approve" (227). He is forced, by virtue of his contact with the world, to accept an incontrovertible truth, the lack of absolute certainty in the realms of metaphysics and nature. He thinks of the consequences of his having forced Patrice to marry Sara and Patrice's subsequent infidelity: "I had thought that my conscience was tied by the traditions of the Church. Was it less by the laws of nature when I had violated them openly to marry him off despite himself?" (236).

It is at the moment of Mlle de L . . .'s death that the dean expresses most forcefully and directly his complete acceptance of relative values in human existence: "Love and hate, these two natural inclinations to which all the others can be related, never merit in and of themselves the name of vicious inclinations. They become it only by the bad quality of the objects toward which we direct those feelings" (310). This is the resigned cry of a des Grieux, one who recognizes that society is shaped by men whose needs, desires, and penchants are constantly shifting and that all judgments must be made from the perspective of this flux.

The Conclusion

Compromise and accommodation. At the novel's conclusion the dean's ambitions for his siblings appear to have been realized. Rose has long been married to the virtuous Comte de S . . ., Patrice has remarried Sara in a spirit that suggests a new perspective on marriage and love ("He came to feel that the pleasures attached to duty are of a different value from the immoderate transports of passion") (357); and Georges, now called Tenermill, has safeguarded the family name by marrying, although not because of love, Miss Anglesey, the mother of his child. Ostensibly there is an uneasy alliance between passion and order, between individual feelings and social propriety. Irrepressible, the dean continues on, striving to exalt man's noble instincts, yet fully aware that men are capable of achieving only limited goals and that compromise and accommodation are society's dominant rules. There is a certain irony in the fact that it is the physically repulsive dean who articulates most forcefully a call to life. He is guided by the realization that inflexible stoic virtue is antithetical to human nature. His is the way of a man who believes above all that man is capable of augmenting his own happiness. And so, the dean of Killerine, clown-like in appearance, preaches a doctrine of infinite wisdom, one in which the practical and the virtuous exist as harmoniously as possible. The wisest man is he who can accommodate himself to the circumstances that will enable him to attain the highest degree of happiness. Ultimately, there is no meaningful dichotomy between religion and the world because the dean's appeal to family honor reveals his concern not for metaphysics but for his siblings' political and social well-being. The dean has learned well the lessons of the world and has shown himself to be a consummate opportunist in securing his brothers' and sister's fortunes. His rejection of all absolute judgments in human affairs leads to a certain optimism, which is, nonetheless, firmly grounded in a realistic appraisal of man's nature. Fanaticism is always nascent. The conclusion certainly has no fairy-tale aura of ineluctable charm and uninterrupted peace. Moral evil, particularly in the form of uncontrolled passions, is a problem with which men have to cope daily.

A philosophy of action.   The dean, a spiritual heir to Pantagruel, accepts that which cannot be changed. Through a multitude of adventures he learns that men are neither entirely compassionate nor heartless in their dealings with others but demonstrate both attitudes. Neither excessive stoicism nor prolonged grief is consonant with human nature, and the need to live with uncertainty is man's unchanging lot. The contemplation of human contradiction is not a source of anguish for the dean precisely because he is careful to distinguish between harmless excesses and destructive acts of self-indulgence. The dean suggests by his reaction to the world that evil will always be inexplicable but that it can be reduced. Envisaging no major revolutions and convinced that the evils of prejudice, superstition, and fanaticism know no temporal or spatial limits, the dean enjoins his family to rise against oppression and injustice, transfers the concept of free will from its metaphysical plane to a moral framework, all the while underscoring the fact that presumption is the greatest source of human misery.

The preeminence of feeling.   Assuming paternal authority for his family in his new role as mentor and moral guide, the dean feels compelled to appeal to principles of honor, virtue, and duty which have been distilled from his religious training. He gradually comes to learn that human happiness is not an abstract concept, meaningful only in metaphysical terms, but one that is real only from the perspective of man's daily existence.

Although, as in the earlier novels, love continues to be the dominant passion, it is by no means an exclusive one. Greed, jealousy, and the drive for power also contribute to the fabric of man's social behavior. *Le Doyen de Killerine* defends the rights of passion but always from the perspective of society, for the passions here come to embody all the inherent contradictions in man's quest for happiness. Passion is violent (". . . I want to say that the transport in which I saw M. des Pesses, who was naturally measured in all his actions, taught me, not only that love is a violent passion, but that it takes hold of the imagination as supremely as of the heart." (27). Passion, moreover, takes a physical toll on the body. The violence of des Pesses's passion for Rose brings on an attack of a dangerous illness. Those who experience passion are unable to control their behavior. The emotions, never pure or absolute, are comprised of disparate, seemingly antithetical elements. Patrice experiences a "sweet violence" when he takes Sara, his wife whom he does not love, in his arms. Sara herself is intoxicated by the plenitude of her emotions and "this sweet intoxication" (255) infuses all her senses. Passion is not only all-consuming for the individual but involves a loss of sense of self. Patrice, despairing of fulfilling his love, tells the dean that there is "no repose for a heart far from the object in which it lives and breathes" (77).

Those who are rejected by their hearts' choice or who are separated by circumstances do not experience a lessening of emotion but continue to feel with the same intensity. Humiliated by Patrice's rejection of her, Sara announces her hatred not merely of love itself but of anyone who dares to express the very word love. Renoncour's movement toward retreat from society revealed his recognition of the force of passion and his unwillingness to attempt to deal with passion within a social context. Cleveland had sought in vain a perfect harmony, one in which the expression of love, necessary to his happiness, would coexist with worldly pursuits, the study of philosophy, and the practice of religious concepts. The dean's vague appeal to honor and virtue in no way betrays a disdain for the world. To Georges's suggestion that he is not fit to instruct his family in worldly matters he retorts that there is no difference between a cleric and a man of the world. With time, however, he comes to understand the pervasive strength of the passions as a result of personal observations. In the beginning, the dean believes that passion can be

controlled through the use of reason. Hearing of Patrice's feelings for
Mlle de L . . ., the dean admonishes his brother for having allowed
his passion to get out of control. Yet all three of his siblings defend
the rights of passion as the highest good and know unrelentless misery when they are unable to follow the penchants of the heart. For
Rose, Linch's refusal to give up his claims on her, although he knows
she does not love him, becomes not merely a particular malediction
that she must endure but the fate of her entire sex: "We are made to
be the victims of men" (70). Those in love feel that their destiny no
longer lies within their control, but they accept this condition as
both natural and desirable and rail out against those who would attempt to stifle the expression of passion through artificial means.
Whereas passion and society remain irreconcilable for des Grieux, the
course of passion in *Le Doyen de Killerine* is inextricably linked to political and social events and is therefore expressed entirely in a social
context. Yet in a sense the conflict remains the same in both works
and involves the affirmation of the individual's rights. Forced by his
brother to marry a woman he does not love, Patrice sees marriage as
the ultimate sacrifice. Similarly, Rose flees to the convent as a protest
against a world that thwarts the expression of individual passion in
distinguishing between marriage and love. The Dean himself suggests, moreover, that passion is a natural phenomenon and that celibacy is antithetical to human nature when he states how Mlle de
L . . .'s charms had a profound effect on him (190).

The prime element in the dean's education is his discerning the
power of passion: In this respect he is forced to admit unequivocally
how wrong he was when he thought that Patrice was ready to overcome his passion" (209). At this stage, however, the Dean is not prepared to see any positive effects from love and speaks of it as an
unfortunate passion whose force he has been taught to know. It is
Patrice who demonstrates most forcefully the power of passion inasmuch as his marriage to Sara only increases his passion for Mlle de
L . . . When Tenermill is overtaken with passion for Sara and undertakes an elaborate series of steps to fulfill it through marriage, the
Dean himself cannot but admire the force of the emotions. Passion in
this work may be a natural phenomenon but it does not result in an
idealization of the beloved or a generous reaching out beyond the individual self. It involves most often moments of self-degradation.
Sara's witnessing in silence Patrice's ardorous behavior with Mlle de
L . . . is a moment of chilling perversity. Jealousy, the consequence

of unfulfilled passion, reveals a sordid side of human nature but is also instrumental in keeping passion alive. The clear distinction between affairs of the heart and those of the mind and the individual's need to insist on the greater importance of the former is revealed when Patrice, weeping in self-pity, speaks of his conflicting emotions and articulates his belief in the sanctity of marriage as a union of two persons who love each other. Admitting that he feels esteem for Sara, he laments that this is not sufficient to make him happy and, at the same time, that he has no desire to hurt her. Patrice thus strikes out against *marriages de convenance* based on birth, title, and wealth and against love as a Neoplatonic convention in which the lovers act out highly stylized rituals but never consummate their love. The love to which Patrice aspires is anti-romantic in the sense that it desires not retreat but rather to be thoroughly integrated into society through the institution of marriage, thus opposing the traditional distinction between marriage and love. Passion is here totally removed from the influence of a Corneillean act of will. Patrice's passion for Mlle de L . . ., we learn, was "the dominant passion of his heart" (266). Sara, influenced by an equally strong passion, the jealousy and bitterness she comes to feel as a result of Patrice's indifference, announces her unrelenting hatred of love and vows to give all her money to Tenermill provided he will never speak to her of love or marriage.

Believing that love is man's dominant passion, Prévost, weighing the evidence very carefully, shows that it gives rise to hatred, jealousy, greed, and self-destructive behavior yet also relates it to acts of tenderness and beneficence. Mlle de L . . . loved Patrice tenderly, we read, but being at once "too sensitive and too voluptuous," she fell prey to Mme de S . . .'s machinations (298). When she realizes the truth, Mlle de L . . . views passion from an entirely different perspective, not so much as an inherent evil but as a symbol of all that is inconstant and finite in human existence as she sees herself reduced to indigence by the men "to whom she had foolishly given her worldly goods" (307). Her repentence for having committed adultery appears sincere to the Dean but, more significantly, it calls into question the passions as an expression of free will and man's individual and collective responsibility for acts of moral evil.

The self and the world; principles and pragmatism. As a result of having observed his siblings' experiences the Dean concludes that "the ways of the world and human politeness had more influence than all the principles" (333). The Dean's basic acceptance of human foibles and limitations is not a call to moral passivity in acceding to social evils. The world, he learns, does not automatically reward the virtue of the reflective sage, but rather nods approvingly on those who exult in the feelings of their own passions and destiny and act accordingly. An aura of harmony seems to emerge from the final tableau. We learn that Patrice has remarried Sara after Mlle de L . . .'s death, and he and his wife "looked at each other as though they were seeing each other for the first time" (365). Ford's view of the remarriage as "an intense moment of love which obliterates the past and promises an eternity of felicity" seems unduly optimistic in view of the undeniable proof of profound instability that pervades the narrative.[11]

Sgard concludes that *Le Doyen* marks a departure from the earlier Prévostean apologetic inasmuch as "God seems absent from the creation."[12] Indeed the guiding principle of the novel, couched in a low, but no less persistent register, is that no principles exist to enable men to explain or control their universe. Man is granted the freedom to choose and must safeguard the dignity of the passions by respecting their legitimacy. *Le Doyen de Killerine* does not mark the moment in which Prévost resolved his doubts concerning God's ways to man but rather a turning point from reflection to action, from an attempt to reconcile undeniable evil with God's unknown and general laws. Thus it is that a quiet dignity emerges from this physically deformed clergyman who enjoins men to accept imperfection in the name of self-indulgence but never in the name of cruelty or suffering and who, by his own actions, indicates to men the grave necessity of always distinguishing between the two.

Chapter Seven
The Novels of 1741

Histoire d'une Greque moderne

The *Histoire d'une Grecque moderne* (The story of a modern Greek woman) appears in many ways to amplify the themes of *Manon Lescaut*. Both works embody the myth of unhappy love as they trace the evolution of a relationship that culminates in the death of the heroine. The heroines of both works, singled out in large groups of women, remain as mysterious to the reader as to the narrator inasmuch as they are never allowed to dramatize themselves but are presented rather in terms of static essences. Their deaths illustrate an unchanging dictum of Western literature, a legacy of the Tristan legend, which defines passion in terms of unrealized potential and never in terms of immediate possession.

Close examination of the *Histoire d'une Grecque moderne* reveals, however, that far from being a variation of the Manon myth, it illuminates the earlier work by its opposing qualities and is, in Sgard's words, Prévost's most bitter and most pessimistic work.[1] For all the ambiguity surrounding des Grieux's return to society, *Manon Lescaut* is a defense of passion whereas the *Histoire d'une Grecque moderne,* by contrast, represents an apology for the demise of feeling on the part of the narrator, whose identity is clearly to be distinguished from the author's. In the previous century Pascal had defined the spiritual unrest he saw about him as the misery of man without God. Despite the fact that the narration of the *Grecque moderne* is circumscribed temporally (the narrator's past life remains unknown to us and his story ends with Théophé's death), the universal implications of the work are immediately suggested by Prévost's designating the narrator solely in terms of his profession and the heroine not as an individual bearing either the oriental name Zara or the westernized name Théophé but as a type in whom ancient culture and contemporary society meet. Nancy Miller lists some of the questions that the title raises: *What* is a *"Grecque moderne"*? What does it *mean* to be a *Grecque moderne?* What's her story?[2] Théophé obviously assumes a more modern occidental name but the tensions of the novel do not evolve around cultural conflicts inasmuch as the diplomat is described as being thoroughly at home in the Turkish language when he first meets Théophé and he himself uncovers evidence later that strongly suggests Théophé is of Western parentage. Miller's questions are perfectly valid but they do not constitute the main interest of the novel. The trial-like atmosphere in which Théophé stands apparently accused, through the bias of the narrator's words, of the "crime" of not loving him cannot obscure the solitude and alienation that pervade the diplomat's world. The *Histoire d'une Grecque moderne* paints the misery of man without man.

The diplomat's retreat from life is signaled in his approach to life as an intellectual exercise in which chance must be eliminated. One acts not in accordance with one's feelings, which must be stifled, but according to tested patterns. The narrator remains in control of his environment at the price of never revealing any areas of vulnerability. Passion, implying futurity, expansion, and extension beyond the self, has been categorically eliminated in favor of highly ritualized behavior in which one's actions are reasoned but not felt. The narrator explains why he is so guarded in his initial reaction to Théophé: "I had formed for her only feelings of admiration which were due naturally to her charms; and in the principles of conduct that I had formed, nothing was so opposed to my intentions than to become involved in an adventure where I had more pain to fear than pleasure to expect."[3]

Théophé's rigid conception of virtue and vice intensifies her savior's retreat from life because it provides an excuse for the half-involvement with her that by the time of her death has turned into disdainful and cruel indifference. The diplomat is ostensibly frustrated by Théophé's view of him as her liberator, father, and god, for the condition of being her protector and benefactor precludes any possibility of sexual fulfillment. On the other hand, by imposing an essence on the diplomat whereby he is distinguished from other men by his absence of lust, Théophé brings into focus the question of judgment, for since he is clearly unable to conform to her expectations of him, the narrator feels himself vulnerable. Like Clamence, the judge-penitent of Albert Camus's *La Chute,* whose perception of human depravity coincides with a period of self-examination, the diplomat increasingly speaks of Théophé in accusatory tones, judging first lest he himself be judged first.

The conflict between ego and passion in the diplomat is not so much his wounded pride at the thought that Théophé could possibly reject him ("Her penchant leads her to love me, but he has repressed it"), as Alan Singerman suggests,[4] but rather that passion represents for him loss of control, commitment, and above all the possibility of exposing his weaknesses. According to the rules of this game, executed in the tradition of courtly love, Théophé's resistance must be lamented, but it is her very refusal that, preventing "desire" and "rejection" from leaving the sphere of ritual and entering the realm of action, must also be desired. Ostensibly the diplomat's concerns about Théophé involve the question of her fidelity, but here, too, he must inwardly desire what he fears, for proof of her involvement with other men would vindicate his suspicions of Théophé in particular and passion in general.

In her final refusal of the Duc de Nemours the Princesse de Clèves admits her inability to deal with passion in the world. Inherent in her retreat is a recognition that passion can be repressed but never entirely eradicated. In the *Grecque moderne* there is no denial of passion but rather the revelation of negative emotions. Jealousy is not the counterpart to intense desire but an expression of contempt on the narrator's part. The perversity of the diplomat's coming to the Selictar's house during the night and later fondling Théophé's bed foreshadows the world of Emile Zola's *Nana*. Like Raskolnikov, whose heart was also unhinged by theory, the diplomat will not allow himself to love. His games have supplanted sexual desire.

The eighteenth century's high priest of sensibility, Jean-Jacques Rousseau, saw in contemporary society a pervasive lack of communication and understanding, a disparity between appearance and reality on all levels. Believing that the human heart is almost unknowable because of the individual's defenses, he suggested nonetheless that it is only in attempting to penetrate the feelings of others that one can gain even a modest understanding of the mysteries and complexities of the human heart. Thus he wrote in the *Confessions:* ". . . If each man could see into the hearts of all others, there would be more who would wish to be humbled than those who would want to rise."[5] The diplomat, by contrast, is content to think of Théophé as an unknowable enigma principally because he is as much a stranger to himself as to others. Paradoxically, the narrator's profession suggests a skill in communicating that is completely countered by reality. He is as much a psychological prisoner of his own fear of the consequences of feeling as Théophé, who is freed from the harem only to have her liberator regulate her every move, even to the point of denying her access to the place of ultimate retreat, the convent.

In fact, it is only the secondary characters who are able to achieve the degree of self-detachment that enables them to fulfill their physical nature. Singerman describes Synèse's passion as both instinctive and irrepressible,[6] and Maria, unable to adhere to her father's strict morality, runs off with the Chevalier of Malta. The diplomat himself, by contrast, claims to be cured of love because of the old Greek woman's accusations: "The force of my evil and perhaps the impression which had stayed with me of such an unfortunate scene, cured me insensibly of all the attacks of love" (272).

The diplomat, who had neither known nor wished to know Théophé, now calls her a "likable stranger" after her death (276). In dying, she passes not into the sphere of the extratemporal, immune like Manon to the ravages of human time, but into a state of oblivion. Her reality is not sustained through the intrusion of memory, her freedom and contingency having been denied while she was alive. Like Camus's Caligula, for whom Drusilla old would have been more terrible than Drusilla dead, the diplomat is in no way able to romanticize Théophé in an afterglow of reminiscence, for she had become for him exclusively an object whose behavior he interpreted as a justification for emotional isolation. The myth of glorious love, as Monty notes, gives way here to a duel between the sexes.[7] Invaded by a sense of the absurd—the individual's inability to exercise absolute control over his existence—the narrator, unwilling to accept the domain of the possible, crushes all potential feeling in himself and thereby severely limits his range of possibilities. He looks ahead to the twentieth century's most prototypical symbol of solitude, Beckett's Krapp, who, left alone with a machine capable of registering the void that was his life, evokes, like the diplomat, a mood of somber alienation.

Passion is not denied here only to be replaced by honor, glory, or merit. Similarly, there are no moments of generosity, no signs of disinterested affection. God is totally absent from the diplomat's world, and the quest to establish an equilibrum between reason and feeling in the manner of Cleveland is beyond the diplomat's frame of reference. Neither does the narrator submit to the ways of the world, thereby acknowledging like the Dean that men are to be defined by their imperfections. Judging himself by the harshest standards, the diplomat attempts to eliminate all chance in his life and must therefore exist in a self-imposed exile of doubt and fear. His suspended state of existence, in which all spontaneity has been eliminated, prefigures the twentieth century's fascination in describing man as the victim of his own capacity for analysis. Seen from this perspective, the *Grecque moderne* constitutes an oblique, yet no less virulent attack on man's rational faculties as an instrument of happiness. Unlike Marcel Proust's twentieth-century work, *Un Amour de Swann,* in which the protagonist laments, years after first meeting Odette, his choice in love, the *Histoire d'une Grecque moderne* is a tale of emotional paralysis. Through the terribly dehumanized figure of the diplomat, Prévost is once again able to plead a case in favor of passion.

Mémoires pour servir à l'histoire de Malte

By its title the *Mémoires pour servir à l'histoire de Malte, ou histoire de la jeunesse du commandeur de**** (Memoirs to serve the history of Malta, or History of the commander of ***'s youth) evokes the image of a narrator who will be a spiritual descendant of des Grieux, a young man whose coming of age brings him into conflict with two institutions of authority, the Church (Knights of Malta) and the State (the Army). Against a backdrop of crusades and constant movement the novel reveals, however, what is essentially an anti-sentimental education, and the pessimistic tone of the *Grecque moderne* is in some ways intensified. Sgard believes that the elements that form the plot—the meeting of the narrator and Helena, the abduction, the tranquil winter spent together, the Moroccan exposition and the return—resemble the structure of tragedy, but adds that "Prévost doesn't unfold a tragedy,"[8] for the characters of *La jeunesse du commandeur* have fundamentally little conflict with their environment. In the interest of maintaining appearance and fulfilling their social ambitions they follow a path of conformity. Beneath the cloak of the Knights of Malta lies a thinly veiled lay morality, relative and egocentric, uncommitted to any principles beyond momentary pleasures. Neither the narrator nor his friends engage in the introspection that might lead to self-doubt. Passion is treated exclusively in negative terms here as a folly which may be looked at somewhat indulgently when it manifests itself in youth but which is totally unacceptable in mature men.

Passion in *La jeunesse du commandeur* is a mysterious force that cannot be instantly controlled. The narrator states that Helena's declaration of love for him had the effect of a thousand inexplicable passions on him. In the world of the narrator inexplicable passion must be thwarted and he slowly learns Perès's lesson: passion that is other than pleasure and amusement must be condemned. Passion is not considered a mere folly to be summarily dismissed. Because of its force it constitutes a major threat to one's advancement in society. It is, moreover, responsible for violent behavior as in the case of Clementia, who attempts to strangle Perès when he rejects her.

The narrator's penchant for passion, we learn, causes Perès great anxiety. The link between passion and violence is affirmed throughout the novel. In a rare moment of reflecting on the underlying disparity between his feelings and his actions the narrator expresses his wish that Perès help him reconcile honor and love. Perès's attitude is learned well, however, and in one of the last tableaux passion repressed but never entirely suppressed, yields to the force of reason. The narrator, attempting to appease the disfigured Helena, whom he has rejected, and her mother, La Rovini, by offering them financial security, tells Helena not to "oppose the efforts that I am going to make to detach myself from love."[9] Genuine feeling, however, has become subservient to political expediency, for the narrator adds: "My passion was perhaps as violent as it had ever been in the most tender moments of my life" (2:146).

Passion as a threat to the individual's well-being is directly related to the morality of what others think. Driven by their own egos to be judged only by what they appear to be, these characters experience a dramatic loss of self in their function as public figures. Within their private worlds, however, they champion a morality based entirely on their individual interests, engaging in great theatrical displays so that the outer act will conform to their audience's expectations. The disparity between their public and private selves creates a grotesque effect, and the narrator becomes at times a dehumanized object whose real self has been distorted beyond recognition. Thus, reunited with Helena after a series of long voyages, the narrator finds her hideously scarred but hesitates not at all: "Propriety led me to kiss her" (2:81). Far from being a golden idyllic period to be contemplated, the past becomes an embarrassment to be transcended. The narrator here foreshadows the world of Laclos's *Les Liaisons dangereuses* in which Valmont, the actor-spectator, is preparing an elaborate seduction scene. The separation of emotion and intellect is equally pathological in Prévost.

When Perès's would-be mistress tells the narrator that she cannot force herself to love Perès and insists on distinguishing between esteem and affection, she appears to hint at a conclusion favorable to honest and sincere feelings. The last scene, however, thoroughly counters this impression. The narrator has sent Helena to the convent with enough *noblesse* "to attract the cheers of the public" (2:147). The worldly narrator, confident, successful, and feeling no need to scrutinize his behavior or question either his individual destiny or man's collective destiny, is able to curry public favor in an act of blatant self-interest (Helena's physical condition repelled him). He stands ultimately as one of Prévost's most unsympathetic characters possibly because, in his craftiness and manipulation of others to achieve a desired social *persona,* he points to the embodiment of crass opportunism and insensitivity, Flaubert's Homais.

Campagnes philosophiques ou mémoires de M. de Montcal

The third novel to appear in 1741, *Campagnes philosophiques ou mémoires de M. de Montcal* (Philosophical campaigns, or Memoirs of M. de Montcal) suggests by its title that Montcal will be distinguished from the narrator of the *Jeunesse du Commandeur* by a more cerebral, contemplative approach to life. Although Montcal does attempt to comment periodically on the nature of human happiness, his growing awareness of the irrational force of the passions and his view of life as an unending cycle of events which unfold seemingly gratuitously, place him solidly in the ranks of the *philosophe ignorant* for whom the mysteries of the human heart are impenetrable. For Montcal, far from being a poet-philosopher whose wisdom elevates him above the common crowd, demonstrates that human behavior is largely determined by the clash of individual egos and that rarely do events coincide with the individual's expectations and desires. The sense of the absurd that pervades this novel is linked to a sense of incommensurateness, of a breakdown between cause and effect, between man's capacity to reason and his actual behavior. At the same time, the very accumulation of chance occurrences which challenge all laws of probability confers Rabelaisian and Voltairean tones on the novel. Sgard believes that tragedy and vaudeville come together in this novel, a mixture that allows Prévost to quietly satirize man's feelings of self-importance. This novel typifies what Sgard sees as an evolution in Prévost's novels in the 1740s, the disappearance of the lucid narrator and the emergence of the man of action, the enlightened lawgiver who wishes to ameliorate human society.[10]

Montcal's designs in serving Schomberg appear noble—to "approach the military profession as something which could be used as an exercise in reason" and to find in love the dominant mode of his existence: ". . . I formulated in advance a plan in which glory and fortune were forgotten. Love alone ought to consume my time or rather always dominant in the depths of my heart. . . "[11] The novel is structured about a series of events in which Montcal's theory about the relative importance of love, glory, and fortune in a man's life will be increasingly undermined.

The violent force of the passions, Montcal soon learns, renders futile all theories of human nature and all long-term projects that hold man to fixed, predictable behavior. Love is no longer ennobling but frenzied, stirred more by what one perceives to be one's neighbor's success or failures than by deep feeling for the object of one's passion. Passion operates in an endless variety of ways. "Love," states Montcal, "is a passion whose limits one doesn't know" (52). Blunting the reasoning powers of some, it can bring out a basic egoism and desire to dominate in others, as in the case of Mme de Gien, who, having declared her love for Montcal, immediately imposes three conditions on him.

Principles are ineffective against the force of passion because, as Montcal observes, passion, capable of altering the best of character, is sudden and inexplicable: "A thousand sentiments which must have been already in my heart taught me suddenly to know love" (40). (Montcal speaks of his meeting with Mme de Gien.) Its violence, moreover, can be directed inwardly toward the self. Learning of Montcal's marriage to Mme de Gien, Mlle Fidert seriously wounds herself. Like Perès, who chided the Commander for sustaining what he considered to be a folly of youth, Montcal attempts both to explain and justify Mlle Fidert's passion by attributing it to the ardor of a young woman. His other explanation, that Mlle Fidert is merely demonstrating the "natural weakness of her sex" is a blatant example of both male vanity and self-deception inasmuch as Schomberg, more than any other character, suffers a loss of dignity and self-esteem as a result of passion. Like des Grieux, the characters of the *Campagnes philosophiques* are conscious that their will has been blunted but are unable to control their emotions.

Jealousy is the emotion that is common to all love affairs in this work. Montcal comments that he was "overwhelmed with joy" when he detected that Mme de Gien was jealous of Mlle Fidert. Jealousy has a terrible effect on Ecke's imagination, making him suspect his wife of all kinds of past infidelities with Montcal. Implicit in Montcal's analysis of the situation is the assertion that Ecke is particularly susceptible to the effects of jealousy because of a weakness of character: "Frivolous, impetuous, defiant, without moderation, integrity, what ideas had he not already formed while in prison?" (368). Obstacles, however, are not enough to nurture love. On the contrary, despair is the ruin of love because it does not provide enough ego-gratification. Montcal's feelings for Mme de Gien, we learn, depend only on his memory and imagination. The feeling of love, Montcal believes, always brings with it immediately a desire for solitude. Yet love is never antisocial. The military life, with its emphasis on public display, precludes any possibility of escape from society. The sense of the absurd in the novel results largely from the blurring between the individual's social posturing and his inner feelings. Thus Schomberg appears at once pitiful and comic when he reacts with delight to the news that his former mistress, Mlle Fidert, has married an *homme de condition,* implying that his own status as Fidert's former lover will not be compromised now. In this instant Fidert as a unique individual in whom Schomberg invested his emotions disappears entirely and she becomes solely an object for the enhancement of his reputation.

As in *La Jeunesse du commandeur,* feelings are directly influenced by social pressure. Love is but one passion and at times is subservient to more powerful drives. Montcal's actions in many instances are not motivated by his convictions but rather by his desire to affect a certain pose before an audience. The principles he enunciates at the outset of his association with Schomberg whereby he would forsake glory and ambition are soon dismissed. Later, reflecting on his liaison with Fidert, he writes: "I began to feel the harm I had done myself. I didn't have the same confidence in all the officers of the army most of whom had too much inclination to harm me" (113). In a society where reputations are built largely on appearance, public approbation is as hollow as public condemnation, and being praised by Schomberg is not a testimony to Montcal's worth but rather a sign of human fickleness: "My name, which had been very odious until that time, to most of the English, acquired thus among them more esteem and consideration" (143–44).

In some respects the *Campagnes philosophiques* depict man as a leading actor in a vast comedy. Montcal, who appears singularly dull, is
able to win the affection of two women and simultaneously at that;
characters resort to disguises to hide their love affairs from vengeful
relatives; Schomberg's self-pity when having to deal with unrequited
love seems unworthy of a great general. The underlying tone of the
novel is nonetheless very somber. Man's immoderation, his egocen-
trism, and inability to control his passions give rise to self-destructive
behavior. Significantly, many of the characters meet violent deaths.
Schomberg is killed in a bloody battle. Ecke is shot to death in Fidert's apartment, and Mlle Fidert, taking the governor's arm, is fa-
tally wounded by Mylord C . . ., the governor's enemy. The effects
of man's egoism threaten the structure of the family itself. M. de Sar-
field stabs his daughter in a fit of rage at the thought that her admirer, Douglas, has more influence on her than her father and he
later kills Douglas in a duel.

The novel, however, recalls many of Voltaire's *contes* in its insistence that every trait of man must be reconciled by its opposite. Confronting Harry Fitz, who has just killed Schomberg, Montcal is
unable to forget that this same man once saved his own life and freedom. Ecke, both deceitful and merciless in his dealings with Fidert,
nonetheless shows a rare display of courage when he attempts to ward
off blows meant for Schomberg. The complexities of human behavior
and the individual's inability to control events from without that affect him directly render untenable all absolute theories about human
nature. Aware of man's proclivity to undermine human dignity,
Montcal, nonetheless, does not portray a world in which all is evil.
At the same time that he assesses domestic bliss with a wife for
whom he has esteem as his greatest source of happiness, Montcal condemns the need to "change everything incessantly to avoid disgust
and boredom" because he sees in the pursuit of worldly pleasures a
denial of the individual's self-worth (478). His repudiation of Pascalian *divertissement* in no way implies, however, a retreat into solitude.
Like the Candide who has returned with his small group of friends to
cultivate his garden, Montcal rejects the contemplative in favor of
action.

In the Supplement, Montcal records with undeniable compassion
the plight of women who, widowed or abandoned by their husbands,
have no place to turn. Most significantly, Montcal alone among
Prévost's narrators appears to have learned from his experiences to the

extent that he judges himself: "My reflections persuaded me that, far from causing me to be applauded by *honnêtes gens,* I deserved to be accused myself of impetuosity and frivolity" (429). Montcal's words aspire then to be more a document of enlightenment than an apology. This suggests that Prévost wishes to convey in the person of his "pensive and tender warrior" his belief that the potential for progress lay beyond human vanity, wars, and vain philosophical debates.

Chapter Eight
The Last Novels

Mémoires d'un honnête homme

With the exception of *Le Monde moral* (The moral world), unfinished at the time of Prévost's death, the *Mémoires d'un honnête homme* (Memoirs of an honest man, 1745) is Prévost's most open-ended novel. In its unfolding of such themes as the vanity of worldly society and the force of passion it recalls several of the earlier novels. Monty notes, however, that, unlike the typical Prévostean hero, the *honnête homme* is unable to find a peaceful retreat or create for himself, like Cleveland, "an unhealthy pleasure of nurturing the memory of his past sorrow."[1] Sgard, on the other hand, speaks of the signs of imminent misfortune that pervade the novel.[2] The alienation and solitude evoked by the image of the imprisoned narrator, a solitary observer of human behavior, an underground alienated man, should not obscure the fact that the *Mémoires d'un honnête homme* is not merely a reorchestration of the universal struggle between the individual and his environment, for, as much as *Manon Lescaut,* the *Honnête Homme* is a litany of romantic love.

The novel is divided into two distinct yet interrelated parts. In the first, the narrator, forced to enter society by the announcement of his father's approaching marriage, is appalled by the superficiality of those who frequent high society.[3] The second part concerns the count's passion for Mme de B . . . The vignettes of provincial society, in which numerous characters reappear in kaleidoscopic fashion, establish the count's absolute and inviolable concept of honor and virtue and his growing opposition to existing social practices: "The Marquis whispered in my ear: They are unspoiled. You can choose and follow your inclination. This community of favors revolted me" (36–37). "What virtue, what good military or civil quality could find itself linked in the same character with such a total disregard for the first principles of human society?" (56). The narrator believes that debauchery and questionable company are addictive and could make him lose his desire for women of taste and merit. At the same time he refuses to accede to an all-encompassing pessimism: "Since I would have weakened my own principles in judging all others by this endeavor, I continued in the following days to appear where I was committed" (27).

Society, the count learns, is an ongoing spectacle that rewards certain modes of behavior. All are susceptible to its influence because "vanity and *amour-propre* are vices of every living creature" (71). Man "performs" in society. He is a self-conscious actor who isn't always certain which role he must play. Having nothing of substantive importance to deal with, he busies himself with forms: "Once this plague of society that is called boredom finds its way into a gathering, farewell gaiety, galantry" (80).

In addition, the count as observer of fashionable society engaged in diversions reveals his already idealized image of women that will later be imposed on Madame de B . . . . "One asks what is the source of such a common depravity in a sex whose natural inclination seems to be modesty? It is certain that it comes less from their incontinence than from that of men, of which they are ordinarily the victim" (151). Similarly, he concludes that women are more victimized by debauchery when their natural grace and acquired skills through education are undermined: "In this weaker sex the least attempt at debauchery is a fatal poison that corrupts education and nature at the same time." The stories of the four women who recount the "finest adventures of their lives" reinforce the theme of romantic love (81–86). The young man who envies the bird being held by the woman he loves evokes an image of woman as nurturer who exerts a positive influence on nature. The recurrent dreams of the squadron's wife in which her greatest pleasure is to be held in someone's arms is a manifestation of tender feelings as opposed to concrete physical possession. The ephemeral nature of love and its link with death is underscored in the story of the adored turtledove which is snatched by another animal. The fourth story illustrates the concept of love as ritual, as idea, which supplants entirely the notion of physical union and a particularized love object, for the chevalier directs his transports toward a handkerchief while being mistaken about its owner's identity.

The narrator's forays into society result in his growing sense of being at odds with this environment. Self-righteous, he himself is a concerned spectator-commentator of his own behavior and tries to cultivate the traits that in his own mind set him apart from the morally bankrupt habitués of high society. Giving 1000 *écus* to Fanchon, his own pride comes to the fore when he reflects that "the happiness and virtue of a girl were going to be my work" even to the point of perceiving himself as an emissary of divine goodness: "I thanked Heaven for having made me the instrument of such a good action" (64). Later, touched by the plight of a family facing bankruptcy, he aids them anonymously. Perceiving that he was "made for a virtuous world," his unwavering adherence to stringent moral principles causes him to assert at every turn his absolute moral integrity: "My aversion to gossip made me always defend those who were absent" (69–70). At the time of adventure he felt compelled to persuade his associates, at the time of narration he wished to convince his readers. In both registers, however, it is he himself whom he must convince of his rectitude. After putting Mme de B . . .'s house under surveillance when he suspects her of having an affair with her husband's secretary, he reflects: "If Mme de B . . . were a slave of a debasing passion, I found something comforting in thinking that I would cure her of it despite her own desires" (113).

It is in the context of his general disdain for human behavior in society that his love for Mme de B . . . evolves. His first glimpse of her is in church and she becomes, not surprisingly, a sanctified image for him, endowed with noblesse and grace, pure and elevated, far above the common. It is her worldly station, her position as a married woman, that at once reenforces her image in the narrator's mind as an unattainable ideal and is a source of unrelenting anguish for him. He is not only incapable of repressing his feelings but stresses repeatedly the validity of feeling. These feelings are a source of vague discomfort to him, a *plaisir funeste* (grievous pleasure) whose source he cannot identify. For in the course of his passion for Mme de B . . . the narrator learns, like Voltaire's good Brahmin, that virtue does not necessarily result in greater happiness or understanding: "What did I lack to be happy? . . . I was agitated by worries which must have a present cause" (111).

Love, in idealized romantic terms, then, epitomized in the person of a married woman who must remain unpossessed, is a bitter-sweet elixir, creating the anguish of unfulfilled desire but sustained in intensity by its very unrealized potential. The "worst evil," writes the count, "is for the mind and heart to feel nothing" (4). The clash between two irreconcilable drives—honor and passion—throws the narrator into a profound melancholy when, for the first time, he questions the wisdom of his principles: "I loved a married woman. . . . Did my character which I recognized as different from that of others promise me much happiness in their society?" (196–197). In a posture evocative of Molière's Alceste he confesses his sense of disquieting isolation from other men: "I foresaw how many stormy moments I would have in this society of men where I would have more censors than partisans" (197). Despite his momentary misgivings concerning the efficacy of adhering to his principles, the count continues to respect totally Mme de B . . .'s marital status. Seeing her in church for a second time, he throws himself fervently into the ritual of romantic love whereby the morbid charms of unreciprocated passion replace Mme de B . . . as an individualized person. The chair on which she sits in church itself becomes enshrined, a symbol which stirs the emotions and which illustrates the blending of the sacred and profane in romantic love: "After her departure, I couldn't resist the desire to sit on her chair. I stayed there for more than a quarter of an hour and I would not have been more glorious and more content on the first throne of the universe" (173–74).

The denouement of the novel is prepared by the most erotic scene to be found in Prévost when, after having been seriously wounded in a duel and losing consciousness, the severely weakened count is so moved to see Mme de B . . . at his bedside that he presses his lips against hers (218–19). The *belle dame sans merci,* playing her role with characteristic authenticity, recoils, a "cruel divinity" who rejects her admirer's "adorations." In responding that he would be unjust to regard her as anything but his most tender friend in the world, Mme de B . . . crystallizes time for him: "Whatever happened, I belonged to Mme de B. . . ." (220). While honoring her marriage vows, Mme de B . . . expresses her emotional attachment to the count in the only way permitted to her—in friendship—and thus makes him invulnerable to all earthly vicissitudes. He can die (physically) or commit spiritual death (by marrying Mlle de S . . . V . . ., a moment in which Sgard sees the triumph of a coalition of religious, military, and familial interests).[4] At the moment the count consents to marry Mlle de S . . . V . . . the absent Mme de B . . . is paradoxically never more "present" because, by his movements and thoughts during the ceremony, the count reveals his inability to give to his bride a fidelity of the heart. In earthly terms his passion is unfulfilled. In the realm of romantic love it is ennobled and purified, transcendent and inviolable.

Monty is correct to question Sgard's appraisal of the novel as primarily an attack on society.[5] For, as Monty notes, in his last round of supper parties the *honnête homme* discovers that it is possible to reconcile social diversion with decent moral principles. The brief ménage à trois in which the count lives with Mme de B . . . and her husband foreshadows the idyll of *La Nouvelle Héloïse* and strains all plausibility. Through numerous examples men in society are depicted as weak and frivolous. Yet there is a compensatory quality in this novel that is lacking in the three novels of 1741. Love is no longer opportunistic or a manifestation of uncontrolled passions. It involves respect, esteem, and sacrifice. In proclaiming the supreme goodness of feeling and in identifying the capacity to feel with life itself the *Mémoires d'un honnête homme* reinforces the image of love in *Manon Lescaut* as impenetrable and elusive, capable of conferring on sensitive hearts a transcendent quality which defies the assault of earthly trappings.

Le Monde moral

The vast scope of Prévost's last novel, *Le Monde moral,* published posthumously in 1764, recalls the methodology of the *Histoire générale des voyages* in which Prévost aspired to assess the sum total of man's geographical history in the light of past discoveries. In his last work Prévost attempted to formulate a universal human psychology and define the influence of instinct, feeling, reason, and education in human behavior, thus arriving at principles that take into account cultural and class differences among the inhabitants of different countries. *Le Monde moral* reflects the encyclopedic spirit of the age, the belief that man must be understood in terms of the interrelationship of simultaneously operating modes of existence, what Diderot was to call "categories of living"—the moral, aesthetic, political, social, religious, economic, and artistic.

The dramas concerning the Père Célérier and the Abbé Brenner, the chief focal points of the novel, are not presented from the perspective of formal theological doctrine such as free will and the immortality of the soul. It is not a matter here of determining whether evil exists, for clearly it does—Prévost includes the most outrageous example in this work, the case of parents who mutilate their child in order to extract money from spectators—but in determining to what degree men are capable of exercising free will and altering their behavior. Stated in other terms, Prévost wishes to oppose a theory of determinism based on sociological and psychological factors in positing a theory of behavior based on self-knowledge, the will to change, and the acceptance of the relative nature of all human activity.

Each of the two main protagonists appears to be overtaken by a powerful passion, Célérier by jealousy and the desire for vengeance, Brenner by an intense feeling of love for his ward, Mlle Tekely. Although their stories are the most extensively developed in the novel, Prévost intersperses throughout his lengthy narrative a series of loosely connected anecdotes and scenes that all illustrate the dualism of feeling and the complexities of human behavior. The conclusions of many of these anecdotes are presented in the form of *maximes* in which general truths about human nature can be derived from the specific incident discussed. These maxims elaborate what appears on the first pages of the novel, a reference to the "impenetrable heart" and the fact that judgment of others must be preceded by self-judgment since no individual is entirely guiltless.[6]

The traditional principles of birth and wealth no longer assure honorable and virtuous behavior, we read. Man must nurture and cherish his ability to feel. The study of books does not prepare for life in society, for as the narrator states, "I had always kept myself far removed from these weaknesses of the heart that one honors by the name of tender passions" (399). Love, the "sweetest of penchants," must be allowed to flourish. When intensely felt, it is the "Nectar of the Gods" (523). The flowering of the emotions is dependent on the cognitive processes. Through the use of reason, influenced by his heart, the individual must recognize and define his feelings so that they can manifest themselves to their fullest: "Time alone could teach me that in the genesis of great passions the heart is as silent as it is communicative, and seeks to spill over when it recognizes its feelings and admits them" (255).

The implications of the title are felt throughout the work. It is a moral world that Prévost is interested in defining, one which accepts man's limitations and capacity for relative happiness. In asserting that charity must be as much a part of the laws of society as it is of Christian doctrine Prévost expresses his hope that society be governed by just principles. The secular world is not in opposition here to the realm of divine perfection but reflects it. Like any reflection, however, its image is imperfect. Prévost exhorts men to be men.

The narrator comes to realize that society cannot be completely transformed but he affirms the need to uphold projected values, ideals which can inspire men to deal most justly with others and thus increase their own happiness: "I read books that depict man not as he is but as what he could be" (194). When the dying Madame Osimar tells the Abbé Brenner that he would have been happier had he led a simple life, her words highlight one of the dominant themes in Prévost's work, the fact that life in society involves a constant struggle between good and bad and the virtuous behavior of an individual is never a guarantee of happiness. Sgard concludes that Prévost views human behavior as a function of competing passions, the stronger one always trying to gain dominance over the weaker one. Sgard does not believe, however, that Prévost sees man as the victim of a blind determinism, a creature at the mercy of his passions.[7] Man is capable of making decisions and his choices are almost always influenced by present circumstances.

Brother Ambroise, one of a long line of clerics in Prévost who have no religious vocation, is wretchedly unhappy in the cloisters. Mlle Tekely, the object of Brenner's passion, plays the role of shepherdess in a charming rustic abode, a semi-retreat from society in which ideals of antiquity are practiced. Prévost does not see moral goodness residing inherently in simple nature. Man's affective and rational capabilities must be nurtured through an ever-widening understanding of the world that can come only through experience. Because he saw a direct link between the happiness of the individual and man's social behavior, Prévost's nostalgia for rustic tranquillity is never a call to abandon society. Like Voltaire, Prévost believes that all concepts of virtue and vice must be social in character. The relative character of all human endeavors is not a call, however, to a morality of feeling. Yet because static, absolute concepts of virtue and vice must be reassessed in terms of changing human contingency, there is a definite strain of the relative in Prévost, an aversion to all fanaticism in doctrine and presumption in behavior.

The Abbé Brenner's decision to establish a new post in Germany occurs at a moment when his passion for Mlle de Tekely is as fervent as ever. It represents his attempt to reconcile passion and the world, his conviction that his existence is defined not only by the nature of his feelings for Mlle Tekely but also by his status as a worldly priest, by his self-esteem, and by his ability to fulfill the promises he made to Mlle Tekely's dying father concerning her education. Love comes to involve sacrifice here, not an approximation of the Corneillean ideal but a sacrifice in the sense of affirming one's interests from the larger perspective of involvement with others. It is thus that the Abbé Brenner speaks of putting into harmony Mlle Tekely's moral interests, his own fortune, religion, and honor. Sensing that he is "no longer blinded by an unfortunate passion," he defines his essence in political, moral, religious, and social terms (593).

There exists in Prévost's last novel a Rabelaisian call to life and to a self-preservation which contrasts markedly with static ideals. If Prévost's social criticism reminds men of their inconstancy and of their contradictory and often absurdly cruel pretensions, it is no less true that Prévost saw in flux itself the very source from which reform and change might emanate. His vision encompasses the ambiguity of his subject. Here as in other works Prévost the realist shares the stage with Prévost the moralist.

Chapter Nine
Conclusion

The identification of Prévost as a pre-Romantic is in some ways misleading inasmuch as his work clashes with the images evoked by Rousseau and Bernardin de Saint-Pierre and their nineteenth-century successors, specifically the solitary contemplation of primitive nature. On the other hand, the division of Prévost's novels into two categories—odysseys encompassing years of an individual's life in which *romanesque* elements abound (*Mémoires et aventures, Cleveland,* and *Le Doyen*) as opposed to narratives concerned with events more circumscribed in time (*Manon Lescaut,* the *Grecque moderne,* and *La Jeunesse du commandeur*)—is equally misleading. For, without exception, references in Prévost to dramatic external events are subordinate to his overriding interest in man's affective life. From this perspective *Manon Lescaut* is not an isolated event in Prévost's creative life but rather a consummate expression of his vision.

Prévost's uniqueness is to be found in his use of the first-person narrative. The popularity of this form in the eighteenth century points among other things to an increased awareness of the self and an insistence on the relative nature of all human judgments. As Rousset and Jaccard have shown, Prévost's narrators are incapable of gaining insights into the workings of the human heart, repeatedly described as "mysterious" or "impenetrable," and their penchant for analysis takes them on a circular, as opposed to a linear, voyage. The anguish experienced by his characters is indeed twentieth century in character. Like Roquentin, the narrator in Sartre's *La Nausée,* Prévost's characters are forced to acknowledge that a man cannot live and know at the same time, and they therefore hope that an order, a sense of clarity, will emerge from the retelling of their adventures. It never comes, of course, and their malaise is heightened by the awareness, again like Roquentin, that "ma place n'est nulle part" ("I belong nowhere").

There are no island retreats in Prévost. In fact, descriptions of nature, a focal point of Romantic literature, are noticeably lacking. The New World cannot eradicate basic tenets of human nature, as des

Grieux and Manon discover. Nor is evasion desirable. The unrest that surfaces on Prévost's pages results from the impossibility of reconciling love and society. In one sense this is an expression of the timeless tension between the individual and society, but it is greatly intensified here by the strength of the desire for happiness and the resulting unfulfillment. As a humanist and psychologist Prévost modified the concept of Pascalian unrest to include social man whose sense of the divinity rarely conforms to orthodox definitions and for whom idyllic retreats, as Cleveland discovers, are capable of bringing about a premature spiritual death. As a sociologist and historian Prévost shared his century's interest in the phenomenon of cultural relativity. His noteworthy contributions in the *Pour et contre* and *Histoire générale des voyages* reflect his appreciation of the relative, but it is the sense of the universal that pervades his work.

Ultimately, it is not the tensions inherent in the individual's clash with society that give Prévost's work its particular stamp but rather the conflicts of the individual with himself, the gulf between his innermost, often ill-defined aspirations and harsh reality. In this sense Prévost is a precursor of Flaubert and the twentieth-century absurdists. The mood of irony, of the incommensurate, is woven into the very fabric of Prévost's narratives. Not surprisingly, the rapid accumulation of events and persons only underscores the solitude that Prévost sees as endemic to the human condition.

Prévost does not merely amplify the myth of unhappy love with its emphasis on separation, frustration, and renewed passion but speaks more specifically to the feeling that desire and fulfillment, knowledge and action, hope and reality are hopelessly out of synchronization. Yet few are the characters in Prévost's world who are unable to accept their finite condition. In this respect there is a remarkable consistency between Prévost's art and Prévost's life. This is not to say that his novels are autobiographical, for they are not, but rather that Prévost, a born survivor endowed with an irrepressible vitality and an inexhaustible range of interests, confers a spirit of Pantagruelism on his writing that softens somewhat, without effacing entirely, the effect of the tragic events that befall so many of his characters.

Rousseau was a better stylist, Montesquieu was more original in his theories of society, Laclos's depiction of the human potential for evil sounds a more strident note, Marivaux provides a more accurate description of eighteenth-century mores in his novels. In the range of his analysis of human emotions and in his thoroughgoing defense of the rights of passion, Prévost upholds an image of man that recognizes man's yearning for beauty and truth amid a world of chaos and duplicity. In a paradoxical sense, then, Prévost is one of the great romantics of French literature, for, while acknowledging both the necessity and inexorability of society, he manages to impart a nostalgia for youthful innocence in his work, a spirit exemplified by the des Grieux who will never again know the intensity of feeling and the rapture that accompanied his first love.

Notes and References

Preface

1. Peter Gay, *The Enlightenment, An Interpretation,* vol. 2, *The Science of Freedom* (New York, 1969), p. 44.

2. In a 1972 article ("Prospects of, and Prospects for, the Fiction of Prévost," *L'Esprit Créteur* 12, no. 2, Summer 1972) Clifton Cherpack, noting that Prévost had become the subject of numerous works devoted both to his works and to the eighteenth-century novel, stressed, nonetheless, that "the broadest tradition into which the bulk of his fiction fits does not yet seem to be identified," adding that "a clearer understanding of the conventions involved in Prévost's fiction will not bring about an enthusiastic response from students of literature at any level without more and better texts to work with." The need for a new edition of Prévost's work, the first in 154 years, was fulfilled in the projected eight-volume edition of Prévost's work under the direction of Jean Sgard published at Grenoble. To date, five volumes of this edition, begun in 1977, have apeared. A 1963 colloquium in Aix-en-Provence, devoted exclusively to Prévost, explored many areas of his work that had been generally ignored, including the relationship between Prévost's novels and the *roman noir,* the comic in Prévost, and influences of specific authors. In his comprehensive study, *Prévost Romancier* (Paris, 1968), Jean Sgard attempted to present an integrated analysis of Prévost's life and work, concluding that the contradictions of Prévost's novels reflect the crises he underwent in his personal life. Another relatively recent work devoted entirely to Prévost is Jeanne Monty's "*Les Romans de l'Abbé Prévost; procédés littéraires et pensée morale,*" *Studies on Voltaire and the Eighteenth Century* (Geneva) 78 (1970). Pointedly taking issue with Sgard's approach, Monty wished to discuss Prévost's novels not as fragmented pieces put together over long periods of time but as completed, published works.

3. Gay, *The Enlightenment* vol. 1, *The Rise of Modern Paganism* (New York, 1966). Gay writes: "The philosophes' glorification of criticism and their qualified repudiation of metaphysics make it obvious that the Enlightenment was not an Age of Reason, but a Revolt against Rationalism. This revolt took two closely related forms: it rejected the assertion that reason is the sole, or even the dominant, spring of action, and it denied that all mysteries in the world can be penetrated by inquiry" (p. 141).

4. Jean A. Perkins, *The Concept of Self in the French Enlightenment* (Geneva: Librairie Droz, 1969), p. 149.

5. In an article entitled "L'Abbé Prévost, Romancier Baroque," *Revue des Sciences Humaines* (1960), pp. 385–97, Claire-Eliane Engel defines the

baroque as "dramatic and even melodramatic, without reserve, with a penchant for tragic overtones, sinister, always sounding the mysterious sides of the soul." Engel goes on to say that it is "often difficult to say where the baroque ends and romanticism begins in Prévost's work." She explains that, searching several paths at the same time, Prévost accepted them all and thus welcomed all the religious, literary, moral, and immoral influences that came his way. In an article entitled "Manon Lescaut, classical, romantic or rococo?" (*Studies on Voltaire and the Eighteenth Century* [Geneva] 53 [1967]: 339–60), Patrick Brady concludes that the repeated themes in *Manon Lescaut*—passion, catastrophes, life and death, friendship, obsession, fortune, fidelity, hypocrisy, and socioeconomic barriers—are counter to the rococo aesthetic and that the brevity, simplicity, clarity, and penchant for analysis in the novel link it to the classical tradition. Because of its complexities, however, *Manon Lescaut* embodies, in Brady's view, principles of the baroque in theme and meaning, romanticism in its point of view and atmosphere, classicism in its form, and "is thus most appropriately regarded as a work of post-Classicism."

      6. Sgard, *Prévost Romancier,* p. 28.

Chapter One

      1. Henry Harrisse, *L'Abbé Prévost, Histoire de sa vie et de ses oeuvres, d'après des documents nouveaux* (1896; reprint, New York: Lenox Hill, 1972). Harrisse's pioneering work, containing many statements by Dom Depuis and Ravanne as well as important items from Prévost's *Correspondance,* has been indispensable to twentieth-century students of Prévost.

      2. Ibid., pp. 84–85.

      3. Ibid., pp. 92–95.

      4. Ibid., p. 94.

      5. John Lough, *An Introduction to Eighteenth-Century France* (New York: David McKay, 1970), pp. 89–132. Lough stresses the heterogeneity within the ranks of the various social classes in France: ". . . among the persons who enjoyed noble rank—a quite considerable number since . . . in France all members of titled families were numbered among the nobility—there were the most striking differences both in wealth and social standing" (p. 112).

      6. Étienne Guilhou, "L'Abbé Prévost en Hollande" (The Hague: J. B. Wolters, 1933), pp. 11–13.

      7. *Le Pour et contre,* vol. 4, no. 47, quoted in Henri Roddier, *L'Abbé Prévost, l'homme et l'oeuvre* (Paris, 1955), pp. 12 –13.

      8. Harrisse, *Prévost,* pp. 96–97.

      9. Letter to Dom Thibault, cited by Harrisse, Bibliothèque Nationale, Mss. Français, vol. 103, fol. 54.

10. André Billy, *L'Abbé Prévost, Auteur de "Manon Lescaut"* (Paris, 1969), p. 40.

11. Letter to Dom Clément, cited by Harrisse, *Prévost,* pp. 162–63.

12. *Les Aventures de Pomponius,* cited by Billy, p. 52.

13. Sgard, *Prévost Romancier,* p. 16.

14. Harrisse, *Prévost,* p. 116.

15. Ibid., pp. 134–37.

16. Jean Sgard, "Prévost-De l'ombre aux lumières (1736–1746)," *Studies on Voltaire and the Eighteenth Century* (Geneva) 27 (1963): 1486.

17. In his book, *"Le Pour et Contre" de Prévost,* Introduction, tables, and index (Paris: A. G. Nizet, 1969), Jean Sgard writes: "Won over by the climate of liberty by this infinitely flexible and adaptable manner of realistic and popular expression, Prévost will go to the point of making his Volume V of the *Mémoires et Avantures* [*sic*] a sort of chronicle, a compilation of reports, anecdotes, reviews of performances in which he will reveal his opinion for and against English taste, for and against the government, religion, the customs of England. The entire tenth book of the novel can pass for a first sketch of the *Pour et contre.* But it is only in 1733 that he set his project in operation" (p. 10).

18. Cited by George Havens in *The Abbé Prévost and English Literature* (New York: Haskell House, 1965), p. 11.

19. Sgard, *Prévost Romancier,* p. 122

20. Letter to Dom Clément de la Rue, cited by Claire-Eliane Engel, in *Le véritable Abbé Prévost* (Monaco, 1957), p. 71.

21. Roddier, *L'Abbé Prévost,* p. 29.

22. Frédéric Deloffre adds that "even if one were to accept that Prévost was living in The Hague by February 1731 and met Lenki a few weeks after, it appears difficult to accept Lenki's having inspired the *Mémoires* before 1731" (lxi, *Histoire du chevalier des Grieux et de Manon Lescaut,* ed. Frédéric Deloffre and Raymond Picard (Paris, 1965).

23. Marie-Rose de Labriolle, *"Le Pour et Contre* et Son Temps," *Studies on Voltaire and the Eighteenth Century* (Geneva) 34 (1965):30.

24. *Le Pour et contre,* vol. 1, p. 121, cited in Havens, *The Abbé Prévost and English Literature,* p. 25.

25. Sgard, *"Le Pour et Contre" de Prévost,* pp. 42–43.

26. Labriolle writes that "the *Pour et contre* is not only the reflection of a temperament but also the expression of an epoch . . . In this climate of political and social agitation, minds in ferment are open to new ideas. They show an increasingly intense curiosity for the progress of sciences, natural sciences in particular. They are eager to penetrate the mysteries of nature and to find in books a scientific explanation of the universe. In another domain, the academic quarrel of the ancients and moderns was transformed into a quarrel of a much greater importance for the movement of ideas, that

which opposes Cartesians and Newtonians. It is Newton's theories, of which Voltaire declared himself champion, which gain ground and which sweep along when *Le Pour et contre* shuts its doors in 1740" (pp. 17–18).

27. Sgard, *"Le Pour et Contre" de Prévost,* pp. 38–42.

28. Ibid., p. 52.

29. Jean Sgard, "Prévost et Voltaire," *Revue d'Histoire Littéraire de la France,* October-December 1964, vol. 64, no. 4, pp. 545–64. Sgard writes: "One easily understands what concern led Voltaire to seek Prévost. From 1733 to 1740 he wages an incessant war against his enemies; whether it is a question of *Le Temple du goût, Les Lettres Philosophiques, Le Mondain,* or *Les Éléments de la Philosophie de Newton,* each of these books, tracked down, outlawed, censured, unleashes his enemies against him . . . Voltaire, who needs a spokesman, will put the *Pour et contre* in the number of those 'rosary beads which sometimes have diamonds' " (Best. 875), p. 554.

30. René Pomeau, "Prévost et Voltaire," in *Actes du Colloque d'Aix-en-Provence,* 20–21 December 1963, pp. 23–30.

31. Steve Larkin "Voltaire and Prévost: a reappraisal," *Studies on Voltaire and the Eighteenth Century* (Oxford) 160 (1976). Larkin discusses at length the question of whether Voltaire and Prévost ever met each other; a section of Larkin's article is subtitled "A mythical collaboration" (pp. 13–37).

32. Ibid., pp. 121–33. Larkin writes: ". . . the two men were diametrically opposed on two related issues which were being keenly debated in France in the 1730's—first, the question whether rhyme was, or was not, essential to French verse; and secondly, the question of the relative merits of prose and verse . . . Prévost was a life-long admirer of Fénelon and in particular of *Télémaque* . . . It is consequently not surprising to find Prévost in *Le Pour et contre* vigorously championing the cause of poetic prose, and declaring war on the tyranny of rhyme. . . . Voltaire was no less consistently subscribed to exactly the opposite viewpoint . . . Voltaire seems to have been largely indifferent, if not positively hostile, to the major works of fiction which appeared during the eighteenth century" (pp. 121–27).

33. Harrisse, *Prévost,* pp. 299–302.

34. Engel, *Abbé Prévost,* p. 43; Harrisse, *Prévost,* pp. 195–204.

35. Harrisse, *Prévost,* p. 177. In a letter dated 1 December 1733, Marias wrote: "This ex-Benedictine is a fool who has just written an abominable book called the *Histoire de Manon Lescaut* . . . This book has been sold in Paris and people run there as to a fire in which both the book and the author, who nonetheless has style, should be burned."

36. Ibid., pp. 162–63.

37. "He is an extremely likable man whose mind is astonishing because no matter what subjects one puts to him he reasons like the most consummate masters of the art and that with a simplicity and modesty that is rare among scientists" (Letter of 18 February 1735, ibid., p. 246).

38. Roddier, *Prévost,* p. 37.

39. Billy, *Prévost,* p. 244.

40. Roddier, *Prévost,* p. 43.

41. Ibid., pp. 44–45.

42. Ibid., p. 147.

43. The most thorough treatment of Prévost's relationship to Richardson is a monograph by Frank Howard Wilcox, "Prévost's Translations of Richardson's Novels," *University of California Publications in Modern Philology,* vol. 12, no. 5 (Berkeley, 1929). Prévost's attitude toward English culture in general is treated in George Haven's *The Abbé Prévost and English Literature.* See also Paul Winnack's article "Some English Influences on the abbé Prévost," *Studies on Voltaire and the Eighteenth Century* (Oxford) 182 (1979).

44. Roddier, *Prévost,* p. 178.

45. Michèle Duchet, "Histoire des Voyages': Originalité et Influence" in the *Actes du Colloque d'Aix-en-Provence,* 1963, p. 151.

46. Billy, *Prévost,* p. 266.

47. Reference to his house at Chaillot and his staff is found in a letter written to Boucher de l'Estang and cited by Roddier, pp. 45–46.

48. Harrisse, *Prévost,* pp. 369–370.

49. Billy, *Prévost,* p. 288.

50. Roddier, *Prévost,* p. 184.

51. Billy, *Prévost,* p. 303.

Chapter Two

1. Henri Coulet, *Le Roman jusqu'à la Révolution* (Paris, 1965), p. 287.

2. Rémy G. Saisselin, *The Rule of Reason and the Ruses of the Heart, A Philosophical Dictionary of Classical French Criticism, Critics and Aesthetic Issues,* (Cleveland: Press of Case Western Reserve University, 1970), p. 132.

3. Moses Ratner, *Theory and Criticism of the Novel in France from "l'Astrée" to 1750* (New York: De Palma Printing Co., 1938), p. 57.

4. Saisselin, *The Rule of Reason,* pp. 47–48.

5. English Showalter, *The Evolution of the French Novel, 1641–1782* (Princeton, 1972), p. 51.

6. Ibid., p. 56.

7. Vivienne Mylne, *The Eighteenth-Century French Novel: Techniques of Illusion* (Manchester, England, 1965), p. 2.

8. Philip Stewart, *Imitation and Illusion in the French Memoir-Novel, 1700–1750* (New Haven, 1969), p. 24.

9. Georges May, *Le Dilemme du Roman Français au xviiie siècle* (New Haven, 1963), pp. 318–30.

10. Coulet, *Roman jusqu'à la Révolution,* p. 353.

11. Showalter, *Evolution of the French Novel,* p. 7.

12. Deloffre, Introduction to *Histoire du chevalier des Grieux et de Manon Lescaut,* p. xciii.

13. Quoted by Patricia Murphy in "A Study of the Narrative Techniques of the Abbé Prévost as Illustrated in 'Manon Lescaut' and L'Histoire d'une Grecque Moderne" Ph.D. diss., University of Wisconsin, 1968), p. 201.

14. Sgard, *Prévost Romancier*, p. 592.

15. Coulet, *Roman jusqu'à la Révolution*, p. 352.

16. Ibid., p. 352.

Chapter Three

1. Suzanne Carroll, "Systems in Conflict: The Work of the Abbé Prévost as a Critique of Enlightenment Ideologies" (Ph.D. diss., Johns Hopkins University, 1973).

2. Monty, "Les romans de l'abbé Prévost," p. 25.

3. Sgard, *Prévost Romancier*, p. 103.

4. *Oeuvres de Prévost*, vol. 1, ed. Pierre Berthiaume and Jean Sgard (Grenoble, 1978), p. 13; hereafter page references cited in parentheses in the text.

5. Monty, "Les romans de l'abbé Prévost," p. 43.

6. Odette Kory, *Sensitivity and Sensibility in the Novels of the Abbé Prévost* (Paris: Didier, 1972), p. 31.

7. Georges Poulet, *Studies in Human Time*, trans. by Elliott Coleman (New York, 1956), p. 149.

8. Sgard, *Prévost Romancier*, p. 85.

9. Monty, "Les romans de l'abbé Prévost," p. 32.

10. Sgard, *Prévost Romancier*, p. 86.

11. Denis de Rougemont, *Love in the Western World* (New York, 1974), p. 66.

Chapter Four

1. *Oeuvres de Prévost*, vol. 1, ed. Pierre Berthiaume and Jean Sgard (Grenoble, 1978), p. 363; hereafter page references cited in parentheses in the text.

2. Ira Wade, *The Structure and Shape of the French Enlightenment*, vol. 1, *Esprit Philosophique* (Princeton, 1977), pp. 203, 249–50.

3. Madeleine Morris, "Nouveaux Regards sur *Manon Lescaut*," *French Review* 64, no. 1 (October 1970): 47–48.

4. Nancy Miller, *The Heroine's Text, Readings in the French and English Novel, 1722–1782* (New York, 1980), p. 69.

5. Carroll, *Systems in Conflict*, p. 31.

6. Patrick Brady, "*Manon Lescaut*: classical, romantic or rococo?" *Studies on Voltaire and the Eighteenth Century* 53 (Geneva, 1967):356–57.

7. Rougemont, *Love in the Western World*, p. 48.

8. Robert M. E. de Rycke, "Des Grieux's Confession," *Studies on Voltaire and the Eighteenth Century* (Geneva) 84 (1971):198–200.

9. Mylne, *Eighteenth-Century French Novel,* p. 99.

10. Raymond Picard, "L'Univers de Manon Lescaut," *Mercure de France,* no. 341, 1961, pp. 617–18.

11. Alan Singerman, "A *fille de plaisir* and Her *greluchon*: Society and the Perspective of *Manon Lescaut,*" *L'Esprit Créateur* 12, no. 2 (Summer 1972):125–26.

12. Monty, "Les romans de l'abbé Prévost," p. 60.

13. Rougemont, *Love in the Western World,* p.50.

14. Poulet, *Studies in Human Time,* pp. 149–51.

15. Joseph Donahue, Jr. "The Death of Manon: A Literary Inquest," *L'Esprit Créateur* 12, no. 2 (Summer 1972):131.

16. Deloffre, *Histoire du chevalier des Grieux,* p. cix.

17. Lionel Gossman, "Prévost's Manon: Love in the New World," *Yale French Studies* 40 (1968):92.

18. Monty, "Les romans de l'abbé Prévost," p. 53.

19. Lionel Gossman, "Male and Female in Two Short Novels of Prévost." I am grateful to Professor Gossman for having sent me a copy of this article shortly before its publication in *Modern Language Review.*

20. Deloffre, *Histoire du chevalier des Grieux,* p. cxxxvi.

21. Wade, *French Enlightenment,* vol. 1, p. 95.

22. Ibid., p. 614.

23. Donohue, "Death of Manon," p. 141.

24. Gossman, "Prévost's Manon," p. 96.

25. Vivienne Mylne, *Prévost: "Manon Lescaut,"* (London: Edward Arnold, 1972), p. 61.

26. Singerman, "A *fille de plaisir,*" p. 127.

27. Deloffre, *Histoire du chevalier des Grieux,* p. cxiv.

28. Jean-Luc Jaccard, *Manon Lescaut, Le Personnage-Romancier,* (Paris, 1975), pp. 50, 173, 194, 220.

29. Ibid., p. 32.

30. Manfred Kusch, "*Manon Lescaut,* ou voyage du chevalier des Grieux dans la basse Romancie," *Studies on Voltaire and the Eighteenth Century* (Oxfordshire) 143 (1975):21.

Chapter Five

1. Richard Desroches, "Prévost's 'Cleveland': A Study of an Essential, Early Pre-Romantic Novel" (Ph.D. diss., Yale University, 1962), p. 21.

2. Wade, *French Enlightenment,* vol. 1, p. xvi.

3. *Oeuvres de Prévost,* vol. 2, ed. Philip Stewart (Grenoble, 1977), p. 17; hereafter page references cited in parentheses in the text.

4. Roddier, *Prévost,* p. 123.

5. Philip Stewart, "Vox Naturae: A Reading of Prévost," *Romanic Review*, March 1980, p. 142.

6. Carroll, *Systems in Conflict*, p. 1 of abstract.

7. Rita Natale Winandy, *Sensibility in the Novels of the Abbé Prévost* (Ph.D. diss., University of Pittsburgh, 1969), p. 388.

8. Monty, "Les romans de l'abbé Prévost," p. 92.

9. Mary Ford, "*Sensibility and Happiness in the Novels of the Abbé Prévost*" (Ph.D., diss., Columbia University, 1971), pp. 10–15.

10. Claude Roquin, *Une chasse du bonheur au xviiie siècle: Cleveland* (Ph.D. diss., City University of New York, 1974), p. 31.

11. *The American Heritage Dictionary of the English Language*, 2nd College Edition (Boston: Houghton Mifflin Co., 1982), p. 1332.

12. Sean Timothy Harrington, "The Quest for Utopia in the Work of the Abbé Prévost (Ph.D. diss., University of Massachusetts, 1977), p. v.

13. Ibid., p. 70.

14. Philip Stewart, "Utopias that Self-Destruct," *Studies in Eighteenth Century Culture* 9 (1979):1.

15. Harrington, *Quest for Utopia*, p. 75.

16. Stewart, "Utopias," p. 17.

17. Sgard, *Prévost Romancier*, p. 202.

18. Stewart, "Utopias," p. 19.

19. James Gilroy, "Peace and the pursuit of happiness in the French utopian novel," *Studies on Voltaire and the Eighteenth Century* (Geneva) 176 (1979):176.

20. Ibid., p. 177.

21. Harrington, *Quest for Utopia*, p. 101.

22. Stewart, "Utopias," p. 20.

23. Ford, "Sensibility in . . . Prévost," p. 85.

24. Robert Mauzi, *L'Idée du bonheur au xviiie siècle* (Paris: Librairie Armond Colin, 1960), p. 569.

25. Stewart, "Utopias," p. 21.

26. Mauzi, *L'Idée du bonheur*, p. 569.

27. Sgard, *Prévost Romancier*, p. 211.

28. Carroll, *Systems in Conflict*, pp. 192–93.

29. R. A. Francis, "Prévost's *Cleveland* and Voltaire's *Candide*," Proceedings of the Fifth International Enlightenment Congress, *Studies on Voltaire and the Eighteenth Century* (Geneva) 191 (1979):672.

Chapter Six

1. Carroll, *Systems in Conflict*, p. 190.

2. Monty, "Les romans de l'abbé Prévost," p. 121.

3. Coulet, *Roman jusqu'à la Révolution*, p. 355.

4. Carol Marie Lazzaro, "Confused Epiphanies: L'Abbé Prévost and the Romance Tradition" (Ph.D. diss., University of Pennsylvania, 1978), p. 2.

5. Ibid., p. 23.

6. Ibid., p. 227.

7. William Mead, "The Puzzle of Prévost: *Le Doyen de Killerine,*" *L'Esprit Créateur* 12, no. 2 (Summer 1972):p. 91.

8. Lazzarro, *Epiphanies,* p. 234.

9. *Oeuvres de Prévost,* vol. 3, ed. Aurelio Principato (Grenoble, 1978), p. 33; hereafter page references cited in parentheses in the text.

10. Harrington, *Quest for Utopia,* p. 123.

11. Ford, "Sensibility . . . in Prévost," p. 24.

12. Sgard, *Prévost Romancier,* p. 374.

Chapter Seven

1. Sgard, *Prévost Romancier,* p. 426.

2. Nancy Miller, "*L'Histoire d'une Grecque Moderne:* No-Win Hermeneutics," *Forum* (Houston, Texas) 16, no. 8 (1978):4–6.

3. *Histoire d'une Grecque moderne* (Paris, 1965), p. 11; hereafter page references cited in parentheses in the text.

4. Alan Singerman, "A New Look at the Abbé Prévost's "Histoire d'une Grecque Moderne" (Ph. D. diss., Indiana University, 1970), p. 58.

5. Jean-Jacques Rousseau, *Confessions,* Book 3 ("Si chaque homme pouvoit lire dans les coeurs de tous les autres, il y auroit plus de gens qui voudraient monter que de ceux qui voudraient descendre."). *Oeuvres complètes,* vol. 1 (Paris: Bibliothèque de la Pléiade, Gallimard, 1959), p. 91.

6. Singerman, *A New Look . . .,* p. 62.

7. Monty, "Les romans de l'abbé Prévost," p. 189.

8. Sgard, *Prévost Romancier,* p. 466.

9. *Mémoires pour servir à l'histoire de Malte,* Préface d'Henri Coulet (Grenoble, 1966), vol. 2, p. 146; hereafter page references cited in parentheses in the text.

10. Sgard, *Prévost Romancier,* p. 475.

11. *Oeuvres de Prévost* (Paris, 1823), vol. 12, *Campagnes philosophiques, ou Mémoires de M. de Montcal,* p. 59; hereafter page references cited in parentheses in the text.

Chapter Eight

1. Monty, "Les romans de l'abbé Prévost," p. 216.

2. Sgard, *Prévost Romancier,* p. 523.

3. *Oeuvres de Prévost* (Paris, 1823), vol. 33, *Mémoires d'un honnête*

homme, p. 36; hereafter page references cited in parentheses in the text.
4. Sgard, *Prévost Romancier,* p. 516.
5. Ibid., 516; Monty, "Les romans de l'abbé Prévost," p. 231.
6. *Oeuvres de Prévost* (Paris, 1823), vol. 29, *Le Monde moral,* p. 2; hereafter page references cited in parentheses in the text.
7. Sgard, *Prévost Romancier,* pp. 583–84.

Selected Bibliography

PRIMARY SOURCES

Oeuvres Choisies, 39 vol. Amsterdam, 1783–85.

Oeuvres de Prévost. 55 vol. Paris: chez Boulland-Tardieu Éditeur, 1823.

Oeuvres de Prévost. Sous la direction de Jean Sgard. Grenoble: Presses Universitaires de Grenoble, 1977–1982. Volumes 1–5 of this projected eight-volume edition are currently in print. This edition is an extremely useful critical tool because it contains numerous notes and variants and has been published with exacting attention paid to the accuracy of the texts.

Tome I. *Mémoires et aventures d'un homme de qualité. Histoire du chevalier des Grieux et de Manon Lescaut*. Texte établi par Pierre Berthiaume et Jean Sgard.

Tome II. *Le Philosophe Anglais, ou histoire de Monsieur Cleveland*. Texte établi par Philip Stewart.

Tome III. *Le Doyen de Killerine. Histoire morale*. Texte établi par Aurelio Principato.

Tome IV. *Histoire d'une Grecque moderne*. Texte établi par Allan Holland. *Mémoires pour servir à l'histoire de Malte*. Texte établi par Henri Coulet. *Campagnes philosophiques ou mémoires de M. de Montcal*. Texte établi par Jean Oudart.

Tome V. *Histoire de Marguerite d'Anjou*. Texte établi par Henri Duranton. *Histoire de Guillaume le Conquérant*. Texte établi par Henri Duranton.

Histoire générale des voyages. 76 vol. Paris: Didot, 1749.

Le Pour et contre: Ouvrage périodique d'un goût nouveau. 20 vol. Paris: Didot, 1735–1740.

1. Editions of Individual Works

Histoire du chevalier des Grieux et de Manon Lescaut. Edited by Georges Matoré. Textes littéraires français. Geneva: Droz, 1953.

Histoire du chevalier des Grieux et de Manon Lescaut. Edited by Paul Vernière. Paris: Librairie Armand Colin, 1957.

Histoire du chevalier des Grieux et de Manon Lescaut. Edited by Frédéric Deloffre and Raymond Picard. Paris: Classiques Garnier, 1965.

Histoire d'une Grecque moderne. Introduction by Robert Mauzi. Bibliothèque

10–18, Union générale d'éditions. Paris: 1965.
Mémoires pour servir à l'histoire de Malte, ou Histoire de la jeunesse du commandeur de ***. Préface d'Henri Coulet. Illustration de Jean Paldacci. Grenoble: Roissard, 1966.

2. Translation
Manon Lescaut. Translated by Donald M. Frame. New York: New American Library, 1983.

BIBLIOGRAPHICAL STUDIES

Brooks, Richard A. *A Critical Bibliography of French Literature*. Vol. 4. Supplement, *The Eighteenth Century*. Syracuse: Syracuse University Press, 1968.
Cabeen, D. C. *A Critical Bibliography of French Literature*. Vol. 4. *The Eighteenth Century* by George R. Havens and Donald F. Bond. Syracuse: Syracuse University Press, 1968.
Sgard, Jean. *Prévost Romancier*, pp. 641–69. Paris: Librairie José Corti, 1968.
Sgard, Jean, "État Présent des études sur A.-F. Prévost." *Information Littéraire* 27 (1975): 57–61.

SECONDARY SOURCES

1. Books and Articles

Actes du Colloque d'Aix-en-Provence, 20–21 December 1963. *L'Abbé Prévost*. Aix-en-Provence: Publications des Annáles de la Faculté des Lettres. A wide range of essays on Prévost by noted scholars.
Billy, André. *L'Abbé Prévost, auteur de "Manon Lescaut."* Paris: Flammarion, 1969. Occasionally anecdotal account of Prévost's life but informative when discussing the events surrounding the publication of *Manon Lescaut*.
Brady, Patrick. "Manon Lescaut: Classical, Romantic or Rococo?" *Studies on Voltaire and the Eighteenth Century* (Geneva) 53 (1960):339–60. A perceptive article. Brady sees elements of the baroque, romanticism, and classicism in *Manon Lescaut* and concludes that the work belongs to the post-Classical tradition.
Brunetière, Ferdinand. "L'Abbé Prévost." In *Études Critiques sur l'histoire de la littérature française*. 3d ed., 3d ser. Paris: Librairie Hachette, 1894, pp. 189–258. An interesting, if somewhat moralistic, assess-

ment of Prévost's work. Brunetière believes that one of Prévost's distinctive contributions was to have placed the concept of violent, fatal Racinian love within the context of a bourgeois environment.

Carroll, Suzanne. *"Systems in Conflict: The Works of the Abbé Prévost as a Critique of Enlightenment Ideologies."* Ph.D. diss., Johns Hopkins University, 1973. Carroll argues convincingly that Prévost's heroes vacillate between two codes, religion and gallantry, that are in conflict.

Donohue, Joseph, Jr. "The Death of Manon: A Literary Inquest." *L'Esprit Créateur* 12, no. 2 (Summer 1972):129–46. An insightful article. The author believes that des Grieux is characteristically manipulating, weak, and class-conscious in his behavior at the time of Manon's death.

De Rycke, Robert M. E. "Des Grieux's Confession." *Studies on Voltaire and the Eighteenth Century* (Geneva) 84 (1971):195–232. A penetrating study of what is perceived to be des Grieux's major source of conflict after meeting Manon, his being influenced by both society's standards, which are stringent and purport to be objective, and the realm of Eros, whose only standard is the total mutual devotion of a couple.

Engel, Claire-Eliane. *Le véritable abbé Prévost.* Monaco. Editions du Rocher, 1957. A rather fragmented study of Prévost's life and work. Presents evidence supporting theory of Prévost's conversion to Protestantism but in general does not contribute any significant information to that of earlier critics.

Gilroy, James. "Peace and the pursuit of happiness in the French utopian novel . . ." *Studies on Voltaire and the Eighteenth Century* (Geneva) 176 (1979). Gilroy contends that the episodes relating to the utopias in *Cleveland* and the hero's search for happiness enabled Prévost to reveal his "sad and tragic view of life," which in Gilroy's view foreshadows the Romantic Agony.

Harrington, Sean Timothy. **"The Quest for Utopia in the Work of the Abbé Prévost."** Ph.D. diss., University of Massachusetts, 1977. Examines at length Prévost's interest in utopic societies. Examines also the importance of utopias in eighteenth-century literature.

Harrisse, Henry. *L'Abbé Prévost, histoire de sa vie et de ses oeuvres, d'après des documents nouveaux* 1896. Reprint. New York: Lenox Hill, 1972. Although some of Harrisse's findings are controversial, particularly with respect to certain dates in Prévost's life, this book remains indispensable.

Havens, George. "The Abbé Prévost and Shakespeare." *Modern Philology* 17, no. 4, August 1919. An informative article. Interesting especially because Havens compares and contrasts Voltaire and Prévost in their attitudes toward British civilization.

Hazard, Paul. *Études critiques sur "Manon Lescaut."* Chicago: University of Chicago Press, 1929. One of the first works to explore the influence of Jansenism in Prévost's work. Recommended.

Hill, Emita B. "Virtue on Trial: a defense of Prévost's Théophé." *Studies on Voltaire and the Eighteenth Century* (Geneva) 67 (1969):191–209. Hill concludes that the diplomat's accusations against Théophé are more an indictment of himself and that Théophé is consistently rational in her behavior.

Jaccard, Jean-Luc. *Manon-Lescaut, le personnage romancier.* Paris: Librairie A.-G. Nizet, 1975. Influenced by structuralism, Jaccard contends that des Grieux operates on two distinct temporal levels, as character in the "time of adventure" and as narrator in the "time of narration." A brilliant study, one of the best that has ever appeared on Prévost.

Kaminker, Jean-Pierre. "L'Abbé Prévost". *Europe,* November-December 1963, pp. 5–55. An introduction to Prévost.

Kusch, Manfred. "*Manon Lescaut,* ou voyage du chevalier des Grieux dans la basse Romancie." *Studies on Voltaire and the Eighteenth Century* (Oxfordshire) 143 (1975):141–60. A provocative article. Kusch sees in des Grieux's departure from the secure, aristocratic world of his father a vertical descent which is symbolized by his involvement with Manon.

Larkin, Steve. "Voltaire and Prévost: a reappraisal." *Studies on Voltaire and the Eighteenth Century* (Oxford) 160 (1976). A carefully documented article challenging Sgard's and Pomeau's conclusions about Prévost's contact with Voltaire.

Lasserre, Émile. *Manon Lescaut de l'Abbé Prévost.* Paris: Les Grands Événements Littéraires, 1930. A rather pedestrian account of Prévost's life with particular emphasis on events at the time of *Manon.*

Lazzarro, Carol Marie. "Confused Epiphanies: L'Abbé Prévost and the Romance Tradition." Ph.D. diss., University of Pennsylvania, 1978. Highly recommended. The author writes that Prévost's work has been misunderstood by critics who have failed to see the strong influence of the romance tradition on Prévost, especially in *Cleveland* and *Le Doyen de Killerine.* Scholarly and written with style.

Mead, William. "The Puzzle of Prévost: *Le Doyen de Killerine.*" *L'Esprit Créateur* 12, no. 2 (Summer 1972):82–93. Mead explains why the point of view and Prévost's attitude are so difficult to ascertain in this novel.

Miller, Nancy. *The Heroine's Text, Readings in the French and English Novel, 1722–1782.* New York: Columbia University Press, 1980. an insightful chapter on *Manon.*

Monty, Jeanne R. "*Les Romans de l'abbé Prévost: procédés littéraires et pensée morale,*" *Studies on Voltaire and the Eighteenth Century.* (Geneva) 78 (1970). An analysis of Prévost's literary processes and moral vision as they evolved in the course of his major works. A lucid, insightful study which consciously avoids the *l'homme et l'oeuvre* approach adopted by Sgard in his *Prévost Romancier.*

Roddier, Henri. *L'Abbé Prévost, l'homme et l'oeuvre.* Connaissance des lettres. Paris: Hatier-Boivin, 1955. An excellent short introduction to Prévost's life and work.

Schroeder, Victor. *Un Romancier français au XVIIIe siècle, L'Abbé Prévost, sa vie, ses romans.* Paris: Hachette, 1898. Very influential when it first appeared, this work has been superseded by more recent publications.

Sgard, Jean. *Prévost Romancier.* Paris: Librairie José Corti, 1968. an impressive scholarly book which attempts to integrate Prévost's life and work. Eminently readable. Extensive bibliography.

Singerman, Alan. "*A fille de plaisir* and Her *greluchon:* Society and the Perspective of *Manon Lescaut.*" *L'Esprit Créateur* 12, no. 2 (Summer 1972):119–28. Argues convincingly that both des Grieux and Manon can act only according to their deeply ingrained social values, which are in large part determined by society's attitudes toward them.

Stewart, Philip. "Utopias That Self-Destruct." *Studies in Eighteenth Century Culture* 9 (1979):15–24. An excellent, insightful article. Stewart discusses whether the weaknesses of utopias are inherent in their structures or are imposed from without.

Wilcox, Frank H. "Prévost's translations of Richardson's novels." *University of California Publications in Modern Philology.* Vol. 12, no. 5. Berkeley: University of California Press, 1929. An informative assessment of Prévost's influence and attitudes in his translations of Richardson's novels. Comparisons with Voltaire are frequent.

2. Background Studies

Coulet, Henri. *Le Roman jusqu'à la révolution.* Paris; Armand Colin, 1965. The best introduction to the subject. Coulet writes with style and clarity. An invaluable tool for the scholar and casual reader alike.

Gay, Peter. *The Enlightenment: An Interpretation.* Vol. 1, *The Rise of Modern Paganism.* New York: Alfred A. Knopf, 1966. Vol. 2, *The Science of Freedom.* New York: Alfred A. Knopf, 1969. A classic, indispensable for an understanding of the Enlightenment.

Mauzi, Robert. *L'Idée du bonheur dans la littérature et la pensée française au xviiie siècle.* Paris: Librairie Armand Colin, 1960. A comprehensive examination of the question of happiness in eighteenth-century France.

May, Georges. *Le Dilemme du roman français au xviiie siècle, Étude sur les Rapports du Roman et de la Critique (1715–1761).* New Haven: Yale University Press, 1963. An important study. The influence of the critics' concern with verisimilitude and morality on the French novel. Useful bibliography.

Monglond, André. *Le Préromantisme français.* 2 vols. Grenoble: Arthaud, 1930. Volume 1 is devoted almost exclusively to Prévost. Provocative if somewhat flowery.

Mylne, Vivienne. *The Eighteenth-Century French Novel: Techniques of Illusion.* Manchester, England: Manchester University Press, 1965. A perceptive study of realism in several eighteenth-century French authors, with a lengthy chapter on Prévost.

Poulet, Georges. *Studies in Human Time.* Translated by Elliott Coleman. New York: Harper & Brothers, 1956. One chapter deals with Prévost. A fascinating study by a critic who has written extensively on French authors, all from the perspective of their treatment of man's changing concept of mortal time.

Ratner, Moses. "Theory and Criticism of the Novel in France from 'l'Astrée' to 1750." Doctoral diss., New York University, 1938. A lucid account of the major critical theories and disputes that influenced the eighteenth-century French novel.

Rousset, Jean. *Narcisse romancier, essai sur la première personne dans le roman.* Paris, Librairie José Corti, 1973. An important study by a noted scholar. In an extensive section devoted to Prévost Rousset discusses the consequences of the privileged position of the first-person narrator, the temporal consequences of this position, and the very concept of reality. An inspired book.

Rougemont, Denis de. *Love in the Western World.* Translated by Montgomery Belgion. New York, Harper & Row, 1974. One of the truly seminal works in the history of ideas. Traces the development of the medieval myth of love as fatality throughout Western civilization. Fascinating and brilliant.

Showalter, English, Jr. *The Evolution of the French Novel, 1641–1782.* Princeton: Princeton University Press, 1972. An informative and well-researched study. Showalter traces the growing concern among eighteenth-century novels with verisimilitude in their treatment of such elements as time, geography, money, and names. His chapter on Prévost is especially good.

Stewart, Philip. *Imitation and Illusion in the French Memoir–Novel, 1700–1750. The Art of Make-Believe.* New Haven: Yale University Press, 1969. A good account of how French novelists reacted to contradictory standards set before them with respect to truth, fiction, history, and morality.

Wade, Ira O. *The Structure and Shape of the French Enlightenment.* Vol. 1, *Esprit Philosophique.* Vol. 2, *Esprit Révolutionnaire.* Princeton: Princeton University Press, 1977. The culmination of a lifetime of research devoted to the Enlightenment. Encyclopedic in its scope and treatment of one of Wade's major areas of interest, the organic unity of the Enlightenment.

Index